Living Enlightened

One does not become enlightened
by imagining figures of light,
but by making the darkness conscious.

—CARL JUNG

Living Enlightened

THE JOY OF INTEGRATING SPIRIT, MIND, AND BODY

By
Elizabeth Cantey

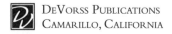

DeVorss Publications
Camarillo, California

Print ISBN: 9780875169330
ebook ISBN: 9780875169347

Library of Congress Catalog Card Number: 2022046439
First Printing, 2023

DeVorss & Company, Publisher
P.O. Box 1389
Camarillo CA 93011-1389
www.devorss.com

Printed in the United States of America

Library of Congress Cataloging-in-Publication Data
Names: Cantey, Elizabeth, author.
Title: Living Enlightened : the joy of integrating spirit, mind and body /
by Elizabeth Cantey.
Description: First DeVorss Publications Edition. | Camarillo, California:
  DeVorss Publications, 2023. | Summary: Learn how to find personal
  wholeness from within, an integration of spirit, mind and body.
  You'll discover that the enlightened live in the world,
  but are not affected by the world. Instead, they affect the world around
  them. The enlightened create the changes they wish to see rather than
  being subjected to the changes of others. -- Provided by publisher.
Identifiers: LCCN 2022046439 (print) | LCCN 2022046440 (ebook) | ISBN
  9780875169330 (trade paperback) | ISBN 9780875169347 (ebook)
Subjects: LCSH: Mind and body. | Spirituality.
Classification: LCC BF161 .C146 2023 (print) | LCC BF161 (ebook) | DDC
  128/.2--dc23/eng/20221212
LC record available at https://lccn.loc.gov/2022046439
LC ebook record available at https://lccn.loc.gov/2022046440

Table of Contents

For Max,
My greatest inspiration,
most magnificent teacher,
and the light of my life...

Introduction

Have you ever wondered what life would look like if you woke up happy every day, satisfied, feeling fulfilled and energized, no matter your age, your bank account or life situation? With the stresses of a global pandemic, the political divide and racial tensions running high, do you stop and wonder what life would feel like free from anger, fear, or judgments? Chances are, like most of us, you have wondered. With everything going on in the world, there has never been a better time to find the solutions to regain health, happiness, and vitality; to let go of stress and release the things that have held you back in the past.

Mystics and masters throughout the ages have told us about that feeling in enlightenment: the feeling of wholeness, of being complete and at peace. What does it mean to live enlightened every day? To live an enlightened life? What is enlightenment anyway? It seems that every spiritual discipline and teacher has their own interpretation. Is it a movement, a state of mind or consciousness, nirvana, samadhi, peace, bliss? Is it religious, spiritual, mystical? Otherworldly, woo-woo, out there somewhere? Is it a place we get to? Come from? One thing I do know about enlightenment is that it is very hard to define.

I have always been drawn to the word and its elusive meaning. There was a time I was obsessed with "becoming" enlightened, as if I could graduate with a degree in enlightenment and I would have the title "The Highly Enlightened" on my resume and after my name. I read books, took classes, went on retreats, and participated in workshops, and yet this thing called enlightenment still felt evasive. I felt myself squarely and soundly in my body, in this time and space, ensconced in the conditions of my life, and not feeling particularly connected to a greater purpose, to Life, to Source, or to "the peace that passes all understanding." I enjoyed the journey, for sure, and the many teachers and fellow sojourners along the way; what a unique and entertaining bunch! My life continued with many revelations and insights, many awakening moments, until one day I became aware that I was experiencing a deep and abiding sense of connection and wholeness almost all the time. It snuck up on me! I felt connected to love, to life; I felt at one with, and completely at peace with, the way things were at any given moment. I knew that no matter what was happening in my body, in my relationships, or in my bank account, all was good with me, and with my world.

You'd think that kind of awakening would come with some sort of fanfare; the heavens open up, the answers to life flow freely, the winning lottery ticket appears, angels sing, or something! But no. My life didn't change much in the external world of my affairs. Most would say my life is somewhat ordinary. But my inner life, wow! There was some major fanfare going on in there! Peace, joy, compassion, unconditional love. Did I mention joy? It was like the dam burst and the entire range of exquisite human emotion was there for me to swim in and enjoy. Living enlightened makes for such a wonderful life, without life needing to change much.

Those who have experienced enlightenment sense and feel a wholeness, an *integration* of spirit, mind, and body. The enlightened live in the world, but they are not affected by the world. Instead, they *affect* the world around them. The enlightened create the changes they wish to see rather than being subjected to the changes of others. What a powerful place to stand in and live from.

How would your life change if you had the feeling of being completely alive in the present moment? What in your body would change if you stopped resisting the events of life and instead flowed easily with the circumstances? How would your mental state be if you stopped judging things as good and bad, right and wrong? If you stopped waiting for something or someone and trusted in the unfolding of life all around you? Sounds peaceful and energizing, right? Feeling and sensing yourself as whole and integrated with Life. There is just what is, and it is all peaceful. When we can sense and feel that we are one with All of Life, we are at peace and all is well with our world.

Waking Up to "All is Well"

"You know, all mystics—Catholic, Christian, non-Christian, no matter what their theology, no matter what their religion—are unanimous on one thing: that all is well, all is well. Though everything is a mess, all is well. Strange paradox, to be sure. But, tragically, most people never get to see that all is well because they are asleep and they are having a nightmare."

—ANTHONY DE MELLO

Why does de Mello say "everything's a mess"? Well, life is messy. Love is messy. Relationships are messy. Children, work, career, and living are all messy sometimes. In 2020, pretty much everything got messy. It's a fact of nature that things get messy… And why does he say that people are asleep and having a nightmare? Because when we are asleep and not aware of our true nature of love, we can only see and experience the human activity, the mess! But when we integrate spirit, mind, and body, we realize that even in the mess, we can experience profound peace, love, and joy. Everything's a mess, and yet all is well? Yes, I think we could all use some of that! The teacher, J. Krishnamurti said, "I don't mind what happens. That is the essence of inner freedom. It is a timeless spiritual truth: Release attachments to outcomes, and deep inside of yourself you'll feel good no matter what." Can you imagine that "not minding what happens" is the secret to living in peace and joy, the secret to living enlightened?

Throughout the ages, Masters from every discipline have offered different pathways of enlightenment. One is not necessarily better than another because ultimately they all lead to the same resolution: a felt sense of oneness with life, an experience of wholeness, and an integration of spirit, mind, and body.

I wrote this book as a condensed commentary of some of the experiences and practices that led to my standing in the light of Oneness. I now know that enlightenment is not a destination, but a journey of awareness and wholeness; a journey with no end. It is a deep sense of knowing Oneness with ALL of Life, which can only happen in the present moment. This awareness is our natural state, but we might not say it is our normal waking state. It seems to come and go, but in fact, it is always present and always available to us. It is who and what we are. At this point in my life, there is a continual feeling of living connected, integrated, and fully alive. And if it can happen to me, and if it can happen during the wild events of these past few years, it can happen to you. Isn't that what we all want on some level? That sense of being fully alive and connected to even the most simple everyday task, connected to each other, and perhaps even connected to something greater than ourselves? To see the beauty in the chaos, in the laundry, in the discord? That is the thought that pushed me, or pulled me, into living enlightened every day.

"As you awaken to your divine nature, you'll begin to appreciate beauty in everything you see, touch, and experience."

—WAYNE DYER

Integrating Spirit, Mind, and Body

An aspect of enlightenment is the sense of fully integrating our spirit, mind, and body. When we experience enlightenment, we live from wholeness, our Whole Self, rather than the separate, fragmented parts. Many of us are familiar with the mind/body connection. We learn of it through pop culture, modern psychology, and even the medical industry. Science has accepted that what we think affects our body and emotions and that our mind plays an integral role in the health of our body. Where most of us are lacking, especially as a culture, is the spiritual dimension. Our mind and physical senses tell us that only the external world of form is real. As if in a dream, we have forgotten our true nature, our spiritual identity. When we are inspired, we remember that we are more than the body, more than the mind and emotions, so much more.

"Ye are gods; and all of you are children of the most High."

—PSALM 82:6

Spirit

In this book, I refer to Spirit in a similar manner to which many people use the word God. I use Spirit to refer to the All There Is, the Totality of the universe. It includes the seen and unseen, the known and unknown. It is the Source from which all things spring and within which all things are contained; the Alpha and the Omega and everything in between. "It" is quite literally the Source of that which we are, and as such, it is not only where we come from, but also who we are, and where we are going. We go into greater detail regarding this in Chapter 6. I refer to Spirit by many names, and all mystic and religious traditions do so as well. Throughout the book, I use capitalization whenever referring to the many names of Spirit. In the following quote, Spirit, or Universal Life is referred to as Consciousness.

"Consciousness is that in which all experience appears.
It is that with which all experience is known, and it is
that out of which all experience is made."

—RUPERT SPIRA

Mind—and Ego

In order to have an objective experience, Spirit localizes itself as a unique and seemingly finite mind and a separate body. Our mind, in fact, is not separate but a localization of One Mind. This individual mind is our faculty of perception in the world of effects. Our individual mind is like a current in the ocean of Awareness. It is like a movement of the water. This current is never separate from the whole of the ocean, but it is unique in its movement and direction. As humans, we are unique in our capacities of mind.

Included in mind are our thoughts—conscious, unconscious, or subconscious—as well as our emotions. I might also refer to this as our mental and emotional body, our memories, and collections of feelings. Mind includes our internal thoughts and feelings and the way we communicate in the external world through words, music, poetry, and art. This mind is seemingly finite in that it seems to be limited. It develops when we are born and will dissolve when we die. It is like our skin and bones, inherent to the human package to protect us and help us grow and adapt to the many environments of this earthly home.

When we are caught up in our small mindedness, we can forget that the Infinite Mind, the One Mind of Spirit, is available to us at all times. Often, when we meditate or are still, we can glean information from what seems like an unknown source; that is God-Mind. When we use our intuition fully, that is God-Mind. When breakthroughs or completely new ideas come to us, that is God-Mind. There is only One Mind and we share it.

It is the belief that we are completely separate that creates a seemingly separate ego, a finite self. But in Spirit, in Truth, we are never separated from the One. The ego isn't a real "thing". When I refer to ego, it is simply the beliefs that our body and our mind are separate and finite entities. The ego is the result of our beliefs of separation, and the ego defines itself as a separate self. When we believe that we are separate and apart from One, from God, from Source, we naturally suffer. We constantly feel ourselves as separated, incomplete, fragile; we constantly look for something "out there" that will fulfill us, rather than turning within to our true essence, Spirit.

When we let go of the *beliefs* that we are separate, the ego dissolves its strong hold on our life, and we can easily integrate spirit, mind, and body. We remember that our life is held within the All There Is, and love, peace, and joy inform all the activities, circumstances, and relationships in our life. The ego is dissolved in the light of Truth. We recognize and remember that we are a localization of the Universal Consciousness which perceives. I use capitalization when referring to Spirit or God-Mind, and when referring to our ego-mind, I use lowercase.

Body

By body, I am referring to the obvious physical body, the instrument through which we sense and perceive the physical world, as well as our body of affairs, the situations, events, circumstances and relationships in our life.

When we live enlightened, we are living from wholeness, an integration of all that we are, and we experience life in a much different way than when we live solely from our mind and body alone. Living enlightened means that we do not deny or reject any aspect of our life, and instead we explore and embrace all aspects. Living enlightened is integrative.

Practical Spirituality

Enlightenment is realizing or recognizing the Presence of something greater than our individual selves in each and every moment, regardless of where we are or what we are doing. This book gives a practical approach to enlightened living, with easy to understand concepts and simple but powerful practices that lead to the everyday experience of enlightenment. This book presents an integrative path to transcending the ego, releasing preconceived ideas, letting go of fears and resentment, and allowing ourselves to become fully immersed in the present moment so we may feel the joy, the peace, the wealth and prosperity, the overwhelming love and divine intuition that is only available when we are in alignment with the All There Is and integrating spirit, mind, and body. Living enlightened is the realization that we are one with Life and that we can experience love, joy, and peace whenever we like, regardless of our circumstances.

It is an interesting fact that we cannot know enlightenment if we do not realize or *experience* enlightenment. Illumination is both a realization and an experience, not just a concept. Just as love is an experience, peace is an experience, and joy is an experience. When we experience love, even in the simple act of holding the hand of our beloved, we can feel *love* rushing through our entire body. It is like the most wonderful drug. It relieves pain, depression, and sadness, and we feel young and so alive, all from that simple touch and that rush of feeling. But instead of the passing experience of random moments of joy, peace, or love, we become the *embodiment* of love; we are giving a tangible, visible form to the love that is who and what we are, the true nature of our Being. If there isn't a realization and embodiment of these qualities, then those are just empty words, concepts, wishes, and dreams. Through spiritual practices, we turn the *ideas* of enlightenment into the *experience* of living enlightened. We turn the thought into the realization.

To realize anything, we have to move ourselves through the concept of it to the experience of it, which may sound strange. I wrote this book based on my experiences of moving myself through these spiritual ideas, concepts, and practices to come to the *realization*, or the *knowing* of my true Self.

The Truth

The Truth isn't something I can tell you, or something anyone can tell you. We sometimes recognize the Truth in some words; they may sound familiar and comforting, and they may sound "true," but all this is still perception. The ultimate goal of seeking the Truth is to *experience* the Truth; then there are no questions.

"If you want to awaken all of humanity, then awaken all of yourself. If you want to eliminate suffering in the world, then eliminate all that is dark and negative in yourself. Truly, the greatest gift you have to give is the gift of your own transformation."

—LAO TZU

Knowing yourself as awake, aware, and fully alive comes through the simple act of returning to our essential Self — our true nature. The insights and practices within these pages will hopefully encourage you to experience your Oneness with the All There Is, the Eternal Essence, in every moment of your life, that you may experience the magnificent, unique, wonderful love and joy that you came here to experience. And that you should experience the Truth, and the Truth shall set you free!

Section 1

What is Enlightenment?

The amazing thing about being one
with the Eternal Essence:
what you give, you already have;
what you want, you already are;
what you receive is forever
expanding and infinite!

CHAPTER 1

Waking Up Whole

Does it ever feel as if you are living two lives? In one, it feels like you're running in the proverbial rat race of life, moving fast, working hard, doing the same things day after day, and not really getting anywhere, or at least nowhere meaningful. And the other life presents itself in those moments of sheer perfection, like when you're watching—no, experiencing—the perfect sunset, and you have this overwhelming feeling that all is well; life is good, time slows down and that peace that passes all understanding permeates your entire being.

Living enlightened is living both lives simultaneously. Except that when we step into enlightened living, there is no rat race and nothing is fast and hard; we are just present in all our daily routines, in every situation, and we feel deeply connected to everything we are participating in. The amazing thing is, nothing "out there" has to change; only our perception of "what is" shifts. We sense, feel, and know that life is exquisite and all is well in each and every moment.

I wake up enlightened everyday. Early most mornings, I practice my kriya breathing and then a quick meditation. Peace, be still. I crawl out of bed in a delicious state of bliss, and I drift to the windows and look out at the unbelievable wild tropical forest in my backyard, with the wind whipping through the palms and birds singing and lizards darting and flowers growing out of control. I breathe in the early morning energy and drink up the last of the humid wispy clouds burned up by a blazing sun, and Presence overcomes me and feels like this—today, right here, right now—must be the most magnificent thing that could ever happen, that has ever happened, and I am one with It. Bliss. Peace. Joy. Enlightenment. And then my 12-year-old comes running in to tell me he has a stomachache and throws up all over my feet. Ahhh. The everyday.

There is a new enlightenment taking place on the planet. It is everyday enlightenment, an enlightenment you can experience in every moment, and this moment now. It is for moms and dads, executives and executive chefs, artists and teachers, students and athletes, doctors and lawyers. Enlightenment, as Eckhart Tolle describes it, is "simply your natural state of felt oneness with Being." It is a state of consciousness where you can feel and experience not just your connection, but your oneness and wholeness with the Eternal Essence and with all of life.

Enlightenment is an integration of all that we are with All There Is—an integration of spirit, mind, and body.

There are no hard and fast rules to enlightenment, of when and how much and what kind of meditation one should do. No rules about what to eat or not eat; to be a vegan, vegetarian, or selectarian; to give up alcohol, or sex, or drugs, or clothes, or the Mercedes Benz. There is no religion or organization to join, because this goes far beyond religion or dogma. Everyday enlightenment is a light-filled state of consciousness, an experience of the All There Is that presents itself in every minute of every day, no matter where you are and no matter what you are doing. Even cleaning up after a 12-year-old.

Most of us have jobs, families, husbands, wives, children, pets, parents; a myriad of obligations and seemingly endless to-do lists of things that never seem to get done. There are not enough hours in the day, as the saying goes. I hear all the time: I never have time to meditate, to pray, to go to church, to even get to the grocery store. How can I live a more spiritual life? How can I feel this connection to the All There Is when there is so much I have to do in a day? How can I go from the mundane to the meaningful?

Let's face it, if the only time we experienced our connection to the All was for those minutes during our early morning, or evening meditation, that would be good. It would be a nice, pleasant addition to our go, go, go days filled with work and responsibilities. But what if we could feel this way all the time? What if we FELT our connection with the All There Is while cleaning up the spilled cereal, doing the laundry, scheduling employees, and calling on accounts? Imagine how our lives would be transformed if we could sustain this connection at the grocery store or while paying taxes. There has to be enlightenment for people like me, prone to procrastination, easily distracted, too busy to join an ashram or learn the rules of a new religion.

Turns out, there is.

When we live enlightened, we live from a deep sense of connection to the Eternal Essence, and we experience unlimited supply, unbounded creativity, and a peace that passes human understanding. Spirit created us enlightened, full of light and love, energy and creativity, wisdom and joy. And when we experience this awesome connection, there is nothing we cannot do, be, or have. The Infinite Eternal created you enlightened, and you are now enlightened and forever will be enlightened. Creation whispered your name, and you incarnated into human form, surrounding yourself with the denseness of body, mind, and circumstances. You may have forgotten your true identity or nature. Your ego-mind and physical senses tell you that only the external world of form is real. While you are dreaming, you have forgotten where you are from, forgotten which reality is Real.

The Forgotten Truth

Why is it so hard to remember ourselves as the Eternal Essence? We become so identified with our body, our circumstances, the mistakes of our past, and our desires and fears for the future that we forget that Spirit is right here and right now. In this moment, and right where we are, God Is; the All is present in, through, and as each of us.

We are the Eternal and the Presence in this moment, and we experience this connection in any moment we take to remember who we really are. Close your eyes, just for a moment; take a deep breath, let it out, and know that I AM. Did you feel it for that one moment? How many moments do you take like this? How many times a day do you just breathe and know that I AM Love, Peace, Joy.

We can experience joy doing anything because it is a quality of the Eternal Essence, meaning it is ours for the taking. You can experience joy washing the dishes, even though your mind might tell you that it is not very fun. You can be in complete harmony driving to work, noticing the sun, the trees, the clouds, the cars, the highways, the complexities of it all, but few of us would put that on our list of cool things to do. I once had a boss who would say to me often, "No one can be that happy coming to work every morning." The truth is, I *was* that happy in *that* moment. I wonder what he would have thought if he had seen me about 30 minutes before.

I was a single working mom and had to drop my beautiful 4-year-old boy off at day care for the entire day, every day. I would bring him inside, kiss his smiling face goodbye, and I would sit in my car and cry for a good 5 minutes, sometimes longer. I would bawl my eyes out. I would allow myself that time to hate leaving him, to miss him, to resent having to work, just for that moment. I allowed myself to fully feel everything I was feeling. Then, I would recognize that this is what is, for now. I would turn on the car, crank up my favorite tunes, and sing and dance in the car all the way to work. I noticed the trees, the clouds, the sun, the trains. I saw beauty everywhere, and I heard joy in the music. I was happy and so very grateful that I had a job. I had a day care that I loved and trusted, and I had a beautiful boy in my life. I allowed myself to *experience* the pain of physical separation, and I allowed myself to be with what is, including the pain, so that I could experience joy for those many, many moments following. Have you ever had those moments of giving in to sadness so that you could allow yourself to experience something wonderful? It almost seems paradoxical. When we choose enlightenment, at any moment we will feel our connection to *all* the experiences of Life.

"Not every sky will be blue and not every day is springtime. So on the spiritual path a person learns to find this kind of happiness without needing nice things to happen on the outside. Rather, you find happiness by being who you really are. This isn't mystical. Young children are happy being who they are. The trick is to regain such a state when you are grown and have seen the light and dark sides of life."

—DEEPAK CHOPRA

The situations and events of the world are always demanding our attention, whether it's a global pandemic, racial or political unrest, or natural disasters. We are called to overcome, to heal and to make whole the dynamics in this country and in the world. But how can we do this when we are not whole and healed in ourselves? How can we bring something to the world out there when we do not possess it within ourselves?

We have heard from a thousand spiritual teachers that "we are spiritual beings having a human experience." But most of us have forgotten our spiritual nature, our ultimate identity. It's pretty darn difficult to forget the human part; the bills are piling up, the job market is shrinking, health risks are escalating, the car caught fire this morning, and dinner needs to be made. The human stuff inundates us and constantly calls for our attention. We hear that "we are spiritual beings," but we have forgotten what it *feels* like. The human stuff is blocking the way to the spiritual stuff!

Releasing the Blocks!

You can't become enlightened, or search for it, or demand it, because you *are* it. We don't have to try to be enlightened; Spirit created us that way. What we have to do is let go of all that is blocking our enlightenment. The mind searches, but the Spirit knows. As we learn to let go of fears, judgments, attachments, reactions, and just wishing things were different, we reconnect with the truth of our being and learn how to experience life differently.

The amazing fact is that while we enjoy our enlightenment, harnessing our inherited power, love, joy, and creativity, we enjoy immensely our humanity. This human experience is meant to be amazing! We are not just connected to the Eternal Essence; we *are* the Eternal Essence, the Life Force. It flows through us, and IT is US. We don't have our own separate life; we *are* Life! We share it with everyone and everything. We aren't victims of life; we are co-creators! We can, and do, create. And we are here to express and experience this Life in a unique and wonderful way. We are not meant to *get* joy, or peace, or love. We are those divine qualities. We are meant to *realize, to make real*, the joy, peace, and love we inherently are. And just as the ocean creates waves from itself which are never separated, there is no place where we stop and Life, the Eternal Essence, begins. We are how Spirit shows up in the world.

Living Wholly

We are the next generation of spiritual beings who live wholly from enlightenment instead of trying to fit some little piece of spirituality into our everyday living. We are seeking first our enlightenment, our true nature, and we draw to us, through the power of attraction and our infinite intelligence, all that we experience.

"Enlightenment is not about becoming divine.
Instead it's about becoming more fully human.
It is the end of ignorance."

—LAMA SURYA DAS

We dissolve the ignorance of forgetting who we are and we recall the faint Truth that beckons us from within; I am who thou art, and thou art who I am. As we embrace our enlightenment, our natural creative state, we *realize* and *experience* heaven on earth. And here's the fun part: It doesn't matter what is going on out there in the world. We will experience heaven and the notion that all is well regardless of anything that takes place in the world, because heaven is a state of awareness, the awareness of wholeness or oneness. We will realize our true power and the joy of living incarnated as a spiritual being with a human identity, fully integrating spirit, mind, and body. We will embrace changes, the differences amongst all humans, and the creative, flowing nature of the Universe. We will live and create as spiritual beings, create as spiritual beings, all the while enjoying the uniqueness of our own personal expression in the human realm, the realm of effects.

Imagine what it would feel like to work, to play, to love, to have challenges and face difficulties, and to feel connected to the Good of Life throughout it all! We begin to transform the situations, events, and circumstances in our life. We go from living in the mundane to experiencing the magnificent! We just don't mind what happens, because we sense and feel a wholeness and unity deep within; it moves us, breathes us, and has its being as us.

CHAPTER 2

Awake, Aware, and Alive

It is said that after his enlightenment, the Buddha was walking down the road when he met a fellow traveler. The traveler perceived a great radiance and loving energy emanating from Siddhartha, so he asked, "Are you a god? Or a divine being?" "No," answered the Buddha. "Are you a shaman or a sorcerer?" "No," answered the Buddha. "Are you a man?" Again the Buddha answered, "No." "Well then," the traveler asked perplexed, "What are you?" "I am awake," answered the Buddha.

It just begs the question, what did he wake up from, and what did he wake up to? Simply put, Buddha awoke to his true nature. The question then becomes, "What is *your* true nature and how awake to it are you in this moment?" Understanding *and embodying* this query is the entry point to realizing an enlightened life.

"Until we awake to the fact that we are One with the
nature of God, we shall not find the way of life."

−ERNEST HOLMES

Awake

Living enlightened is awakening to our true wholeness and
our true nature. We are now called to be fully awake to
everything about us, our human self and our spiritual nature,
our Oneness and Wholeness. Can you *hear* that call? Can
you feel the divine tug on your heart? That is how you'll
know the portal to living an enlightened life is beginning
to open. How do we wake up and stay awake in a world of
full of apathy? Do we even know what it means to be fully
awake to everything about us?

Most of us are very awake to certain aspects about our
being. We are fully awake to the pressures of daily living in a
pandemic, the loss of lifestyle and freedoms and income, the
toll of aging on our bodies, the demands of family, and the IRS.
We are awake in the sense that we are not comfortably asleep
in our beds, but are we awake to our true Nature? Sometimes,
we are so busy living in the external world of circumstances,
events, and relationships that we forget how to live from our
Source, from Spirit, love, peace, creativity, and power.

When we live from the inside out, we bring our awareness
into each and every situation, rather than allowing the situations
and events dictate how we think and feel, bringing unhappiness
and stress. The practice is to bring our internal awareness of the
oneness with Life into each and every moment.

Being awake, aware, and truly alive is living in ultimate Wholeness. We are fully integrating spirit, mind, and body. Every mystic tradition teaches us that we are One with Life, and yet here we are in these bodies, with our finite mind telling us we are different, separate and apart from all of life. How do we reconcile feeling separate with being Whole?

Reality vs reality

We begin by recognizing there is the reality of the external world of form, the world of situations, events, and circumstances. However, we realize that all the conditions in our life are temporary. Nothing in form will last, even the sun, the moon, the stars; all of it will constantly change and grow until it withers and dies, making way for new forms. Our satisfaction from these temporary things and situations in our life is also fleeting, because as the forms come and go, so does our satisfaction with them.

When we live from the outside in, we feel unfulfilled and unsatisfied because we attach so much importance to all the things that are fleeting. When we live from the outside in, we feel separated from each other. It's like we just can't get close enough, intimate enough with others to break this feeling of loneliness and disconnection. Our mind will constantly tell us we are not like them; they are different, and we are alone. We struggle to find wholeness in relationships, family, work, and most of our endeavors. And the struggle becomes more and more real under the increasing pressure of the threat to our health, to our economy, and to our very way of living. At some point, sooner or later, Life demands that we find an inner solution which is grounded in another Reality.

There is a changeless Reality, the Eternal, the Infinite. Have you felt that in your heart, that there is something so big and so real we are unable to even define it, much less understand it? Have you felt you were a part of It? We experience it in some moments, and we feel so alive!

We have called this Changeless Reality by many names, seen it expressed in many cultures and spoken about in many languages. Most often, here in North America, we use the word God. Many of us, myself included, have grown up with the concept of God as a force and power outside ourself. There is the god with the white beard, sitting on a throne up in the sky, judging, reacting, approving or disapproving; but God is so much more than a man and so much more than a concept.

"You must forget everything you have ever learned about God. It won't help you. It may comfort you, but such comfort is imaginary; it is an illusion. Let go of all the false comforts of the mind. When you let all images, all concepts, all hopes, and all beliefs end, Stillness is experienced. Experience the core of Stillness. Dive into it and surrender fully. In full surrender to Stillness, you directly experience That to which the concept of God points. In that direct experience, you awaken from the dream of the mind and realize that the concept of God points to who you truly are."

—ADYASHANTI

When we awaken, we move beyond words, beyond concepts and into the very essence of Stillness itself. In the silence we recognize that Spirit is the essence of all Life and our life, of all Love and our love, and all Power and our power. We wake up to the fact that, like the rays of light emanating from the sun, we are pure unadulterated emanations of Spirit. We and our Father, the Creator, are one. When we realize we are the divine emanations of Infinite Spirit, we wake up to our true Nature. We wake up to this incredible divine partnership every day.

"We must awaken to the realization that a divine partnership has already been formed between the seen and the unseen, between the visible and the invisible."

—ERNEST HOLMES

We may recognize we are not all that God is, for God is present in and as all of life in the universe. However, we can say that all of God, every divine aspect of Spirit, is who we are. Spirit as awareness does not divide Itself into bits and pieces, a piece for me and a piece for you. Consciousness is wholly present and available in, through, and as every one of us, just as the rays of the sun are the sun itself, not bits and pieces of the sun.

Because all of Spirit is who we are, we can choose which aspects of Spirit we wish to express in our lives; Love, as the mother or father; Joy, as the dancer; Creativity, as the artist; Peace, as the meditator; Organization, as the scientist; Health, as the doctor or healer; Wealth, as the business person;

or any other aspects of the Divine. Most of us choose a unique combination of qualities to express ourselves. We are each unique, and as we identify with the eternal qualities of Spirit, we are eternally satisfied. These qualities do not come and go as things and situations do, but they deepen and expand as we continue to integrate them in our lives.

When we live our lives from the outside in, we are living from one circumstance to the next. We get bounced around from event to event, from feeling to feeling, and from thought to thought. We are victims of circumstances, whether they are good or bad, and we will always feel separated. But when we live from our Spiritual Reality, from the inside or "insight" out, we integrate spirit, mind, and body and feel whole. We awake to our Whole Nature and the truth of our Being.

Aware

Mystics have taught that we are to become aware of our Oneness, Oneness with Life, or what we call the Ultimate Reality, and our Oneness with all of humanity.

There is no great thing we need to do to make this happen, no new wisdom to learn or years of spiritual practices; it is a matter of shifting our focus and attention. We simply become tuned in to this Ultimate Reality which is always present right now, in this moment. Have you ever asked yourself, if we already are One, then why is so hard to realize it, to become aware of it and live it? The answer lies in what we believe is real.

We live as if the world of effects is the one true Cause of all things. Science still teaches that only what we can examine through our senses is real; only what we can measure and manipulate is real. If we can't see it, measure it, manipulate it, then it doesn't exist. Science discounts entirely what the Greeks called Sophia, or inner wisdom, even though Einstein himself said, "Reality is merely an illusion, albeit a very persistent one." Science does not acknowledge a Unified Divine Source from which all things emanate (yet).

"Enlightenment depends to a large extent on believing that you are born for Freedom in this lifetime, and that it is available now, in this moment. The mind, which creates the past and future, keeps you out of the moment where the Truth of your Being can be discovered. In this moment, there is always Freedom and there is always peace. Stay in the moment, and dare to consider that you can be free now."

—ADYASHANTI

Our human mind, the ego-mind, is wonderful in the world of effects; with it, we can function well in our everyday lives, jobs, and relationships. But it is our connection with One Mind that gives us true wisdom and creative insight. When we depend solely on the ego-mind, we are able to live only a fraction of our truth, and we can only experience life as a victim of our circumstances. Even the best circumstances will never satisfy our urge to realize our Wholeness and Oneness. To live our life fully and freely, we reinforce the divine connection with the Source of our being, Spirit within us. There is that ever-present urge or call to wake up whole. Do you hear it, sense it, feel it?

Can you hear yourself thinking right now? What is the next thought that comes to your mind? You can become aware of your thoughts, right? This awareness is much closer to who we really are, the Source of our being, than the thought itself. The ego-mind is the thought. Source Mind is the consciousness, or Self, that is aware of the thought. When we live integrated and connected, we can experience both, and understand what is Real and what is passing. The true Self is the consciousness that watches the thoughts and emotions that pass through the mind. The good news is that as we are aware of what is passing through, or camping out, in our ego-mind, we can change it! We finally gain a sense of freedom from our limiting thoughts, our limited self, and step into Wholeness—our enlightened and creative Self.

"To know yourself as the Being underneath the thinker, the stillness underneath the mental noise, the love and joy underneath the pain, is freedom, salvation, enlightenment."

—ECKHART TOLLE

The enlightened live from this Ultimate Reality and not from what appears to be real to the ego, the transient forms that come and go in our life. This is the essence of every mystical tradition. "Nothing real can be threatened. Nothing unreal exists. Herein lies the peace of God," states *A Course in Miracles*. Krishna, from the Bhagavad Gita, said, "That which is real is always real. That which is unreal is always unreal. The person who knows the truth, knows the difference." And the Tao Te Ching says, "Wise are they that center their hearts on the inner essence of the things, and not on outer appearances." We are called from within to discover the Truth of our Being. We are called to wake up. There has never been a more urgent call to understand Wholeness and to live enlightened.

The question becomes *how* do we connect with our Divine Self, integrate our spirit, mind, and body? There are two aspects to answer this question: One, by becoming aware of the Truth within, and two, by becoming aware of the false conditioning from without; that is what this book is about.

"Who looks outside, dreams. Who looks inside, awakens."

—CARL JUNG

Alive

The path of enlightenment is transformational. It is experiencing what is on the human plane, on this earth, in this body, from a spiritual perspective, as a spiritual being, so we may transform any experience from a seemingly limited one into an unlimited one; we transform the mundane into the miraculous. We transform everyday experiences into enlightened ones. Enlightenment is our natural creative state, a state of simple connection with the Divine within ourselves and all things. When we are fully present and alive in all we do, we sense and feel the world around us as alive with the Eternal Essence, and we are connected and whole. Fully alive means fully integrating spirit, mind, and body.

Enlightenment in a Coffee Cup

One afternoon, I was doing the dishes. I was peaceful, content, happy at the warm running water, enjoying my handmade turquoise dishes, grateful for the quiet beauty of the garden outside the window. Nothing amazing, but all in all a pleasant experience. I was present, in the moment. As I was gazing out the window, watching the breeze blow through the palms, rinsing a coffee cup, I could hear the voice of a hundred spiritual masters whisper in my ear, as they had done a thousand times before, "You are what you are looking for." Time seemed to stop. I almost dropped the cup. "So stop looking!" the voice added for emphasis. I heard it. My body heard it, and my mind, my soul, and my Spirit heard it. Time sped up. I looked outside at the illuminated garden teeming with life, and I looked at the coffee cup I was rinsing, and I knew in that instant, yes, I AM. I AM what I have been looking for: Joy, Peace, Unconditional Love, Abundance, Health, Wealth, and Well-Being. Oh. My. Gosh—I AM WHAT I AM LOOKING FOR!!! Honestly, I wanted to fall to my knees and weep with joy but I only had three and a half minutes to finish washing the dishes and pick up my son from the bus stop.

"You are already that which you seek."

−RAMANA MAHARSHI

It was that simple. It IS that simple. Every day. Doing the dishes, the laundry, organizing a meeting. In between every thought, on every breath, in every moment, we can realize we are not just connected to the Divine, but we are the Divine expressed. Everything we do is a spiritual endeavor and not just a human one; every activity becomes the activity of joy, rather than a means to get to the next activity. Often, we rush to finish the next thing and then the next, so we can finally relax and have some "peace" sometime in the future. Why not relax now? Why not rest in one perfect moment while washing the dishes, ordering takeout, or planning the next sales call?

When we experience the All There Is in everything we do, we're not *waiting* to find peace, joy, and presence later, at some time in the future, when we finish what we are doing now. We *enjoy* and *experience peace* doing the dishes, driving, managing spreadsheets, and taking meetings now. In this state of consciousness, someone canceling an appointment or changing a meeting won't bother us. We will just say, "oh," and move to the next thing on our to-do list with an unexplained smile on our face. We have the presence, energy, and vitality to move with the flow of life, rather than fight against it.

The world of form, all the events, circumstances, things, and relationships in our life, will change and grow and fade away. In and of themselves, they will never satisfy us. When we wake up to our true nature, we become aware of the peace, harmony, and joy that is available in each moment, in every activity. We don't wait for serenity; we allow it to flow through us and into every aspect of our lives. Enlightenment is the consciousness in which we experience our Oneness, beyond belief, beyond knowing; it is a felt, intuitive, innate Oneness with All There Is. We must also remember, All There

Is includes the dishes, laundry, running a multimillion-dollar company, and putting the kids to sleep. Enlightenment exists in this moment, now.

CHAPTER 3

Be Here Now

Why, in those fleeting moments watching a sunset or looking into your child's eyes, the exhilaration of rafting down a class 4 river, or gazing into the miracle of a snowflake, does life feel so complete, so blissful? Perhaps it's because in those moments, we become fully present.

Perfect Moments

Our whole being, the spiritual Self and the human self with all of its senses, can feel the wholeness and the uniqueness of perfect moments. We are fully integrated as spirit, mind, and body. We intuit the presence of Creation in that moment, and it heightens our senses. We can smell the crispness of the air, see the beauty radiating from the sky, and feel the power of the sun's warmth on our cheek. We are completely alive in that moment.

It is easy to brush those moments off as special, as different, and as unsustainable in our "real life." What if that was our real life? What if we could feel and sense that wholeness, that *alive-ness,* whenever we choose? I believe we can, and we will, as we become fully present in every moment. Perfect moments are simply moments in which we are fully present.

"All power resides in the present moment because it is the only moment that exists. Resistance to the present moment creates suffering, a continual feeling of unease, alienation, thoughts of not belonging, or wishing things were different, or I'll be happy when... but the illusory future we dream of never arrives."

—ECKHART TOLLE

The Past and the Future

There is no past. It doesn't exist as a place you can go. It is only a collection of memories, thoughts, and perceptions of some event. There is no future. We all know that tomorrow never comes. The future is a projection of what we think may happen, or could happen, or could never happen. None of our thoughts about the future make it so. We cannot visit the future or change it by dumping our worry and anxiety onto it. There is only this moment right now.

When we place our attention on the past or the future, we are not placing our attention on something real; we are thinking thoughts *about* the past or *about* the future, but we are *experiencing* our thoughts about the past or the future in this present moment, right now. Yet, we cannot experience the fullness of the present moment, this moment now, when we allow our minds to dwell on those thoughts of the past or the future. Jesus, a master teacher of enlightenment, said the kingdom of Heaven is at hand now. The kingdom of Heaven is not a place; you cannot find it with signs or Google Maps. It is an enlightened state of awareness. The experience of enlightenment is available in this moment as soon as we allow ourselves to realize it. He also taught the kingdom of Heaven is within; it occurs when we turn our attention inward.

What we call miraculous happens when we recognize (remember) who and what we really are. The mundane appears only when we are trapped in our limited ways of thinking, stuck in old habits or mindsets. We may seem to experience the mundane more often only because we spend more time in our small-mindedness, our ego-mind, with thoughts running rampant, with our focus on the past or the future, or simply resisting what is already taking place. Now, this moment, is the point of power and transformation. Now is when we can choose to become fully aware of both our humanity and our divinity. Now we can turn within and experience the vast spaciousness of silence and creativity. Now we are free and fully integrated. The past and the future are concepts. They don't actually exist.

Being Fully Present

Have you noticed that the term "mindful" has become quite common in the last decade or so? Is it a practice? A way of life? A mind that's full or empty? When I think of being mindful and living in mindfulness, it brings to my mind (pun intended) those synchronized moments of wholeness and oneness, like experiencing perfect peace while gazing into a crackling fire or feeling blissfully whole watching the ocean waves roll in. When I brought my meditation practices into my everyday life, I became more mindful. Honestly, one of the best benefits of being mindful was not losing my car keys ever again. Living enlightened everyday has its perks! When I am attentive and fully present in any given moment, there is something wonderful in that moment, a present, a gift, an awareness of something beautiful, and it feels like it is there just for me. I can be walking the dog and see the osprey fly from its nest for the first time, which fills me with awe and wonder. Or making a cup of coffee and being aware of the entire universe in the smell of the coffee. Not only can I sense and experience the beauty in the many moments of my seemingly ordinary life, but when I am aware of being the consciousness behind the thoughts that race through my mind, I am also aware; *I can stop them.*

How Often are You Using Your Mind? How Often is Your Mind Using You?

When I was very young and my mom would ask me to stop shaking my leg in church, giving everyone in the pew an unwelcome frantic vibrational massage, I would answer, "I can't help it." She would snap back, "If you can't help it, who can?" Hmmmmm. That's a Buddhist koan, I'm sure. Who was it that could stop my leg from shaking? I had to think about that as a young child, and I eventually came to the conclusion that I must be the one who could help it. And that is my earliest practice of mindfulness! My mom must have been a Zen master in a previous life.

More often than not, our minds are using us, and we have forgotten who is in control. Just like the child who believes her actions are uncontrollable, we have succumbed to the idea that our thoughts are beyond our control and there is nothing to be done about them. In Reality, when we live from the Self, from the inside out, we experience Presence and Wholeness; the ego-mind relaxes, and we experience peace.

There are two simple ways I use to become fully present, or mindful. I turn my attention to some aspect of my inner life, or I turn my complete attention to what is happening around me.

In the first case, I can look at my breath; I ask myself, how am I breathing? I wait. I feel the breath short and stuck in my chest and I purposefully breathe deeply, pulling it into my belly. Or I feel the sensation as the air comes through my nose and down my throat, filling my lungs. Another practice is to become intensely aware of the sensations in my body. You can do this right now. How do your feet feel resting on the floor, or curled up under you? What is the sensation? What is the feeling in your legs, thighs, and hips? Just notice. What is going on in your stomach? Is it full, empty, rumbling, still? What is the feeling in your arms? Your neck? Your shoulders, your head? When we want to become fully present to ourselves, we can use these simple techniques.

Sometimes I turn my attention and focus to what is outside of me and I play a little game I call, "Just the facts, Ma'am", which is from an old tv show when I was a child. There was a detective who would interview the hysterical person who had just witnessed a crime, and to cut through the hysteria, the judgments, and the opinions, he would say,

"Just the facts, ma'am." When my mind wanders, and I want to cut through the cacophony of voices in my head, I just turn my attention to the room, or the road, or the meeting, and just state what is, only the facts. There is a white bookcase. The ceilings are high. They are white. The chairs are all blue. Except one. It's grey. This technique can help us stay focused on what is happening in this moment and keep our thoughts from racing. As we will discover in the chapters that follow, our ego wants complete control, and when it has control, we cannot live from our Wholeness, we cannot experience our Oneness. The ego or body-mind can only sense separation.

We are the Light

One afternoon, after a rather uneventful morning meditation, I swung my legs over the edge of the bed to get up and go about my day. But before my feet hit the floor, I had this amazing experience. I was sensing myself as pure light. I was at the center, and this incredible bright light spread out from me and connected every molecule of my being with every molecule of life everywhere. The only words I can use to describe it was like an intricate web of brilliant light-streams, billions of them pouring from me and pulsing through me and radiating away from me. It was amazing and profound. Even more amazing was that I could sense this light was Love Itself. I felt myself as "the light of the world" and those words came to me right after.

This is the light that lights up every man, woman, and child. It holds us and loves us and fills us up with Itself. There is nothing we do to deserve it or earn it; we ARE It.

This Love and Light embraced me and connected me to All. I could experience mySelf as one with All... I didn't know it then, but the practices in this book would lead me to continue having these wonderful, transformative experiences of being connected to the All There Is by this beautiful, loving, pure Light.

"You are the light of the world. A city set on a hill cannot be hidden. Neither do men light a lamp, and put it under a bushel. Instead they put it on a stand, and it gives light to everyone in the house. In the same way, let your light shine before everyone, that they may see your good deeds and praise your Father in heaven."

—MATTHEW 5:14–16

You are the light of the world and there is nothing else you can be, because the Eternal Essence created you as Itself, in its own nature. Everything else that you think you are or are not is only a thought. It is something the ego made up about you to hold on to its small identity. The ego is your human animal identity, while enlightenment is your spiritual Source identity. We are, after all, human animals and spiritual Beings, human Beings.

When we go within to the silent place of the Most High, we know and experience our Self without thought, without boundaries, without judgments, without precedent. We feel ourselves as we truly are: Light, Love, and Peace, enlightened. We feel and know our divine connection with everyone, everything, the All of Life. The clouds and thick fog that surround our personal circumstances lift and we experience life as it is meant to be lived, with the eternal Light always shining; in unconditional Love, a love that does not come and go as an emotion, but permeates every aspect of our life; in Peace that passes human understanding; and in an exquisite Joy that is never affected by external circumstances. Enlightenment, then, is being completely and fully present right where we are, doing exactly what we are doing, being with whoever we are with, and sensing and shining our light of Oneness and Wholeness.

CHAPTER 4

The Ego and Enlightenment

What is in the way of us sensing and shining our light in every circumstance? Of realizing or staying present in this state of consciousness? Most of us are only aware of our life in 3D. We are often painfully aware of our seemingly limited and finite human existence, rather than our full and wholly integrated existence. Our ego, our limited human identity, has been running the show.

We have forgotten who or what we essentially
are and have mistaken ourself instead for a collection
of thoughts, images, memories, feelings,
sensations, and perceptions.

—RUPERT SPIRA

What is Ego?

The ego, as we are using the term in this book, is our limited human identity, our animal mind. We are animals after all! It is the mind that thinks that it is a separate and finite being, a body and mind that has come into this world and will die and leave it. It is counterfeit because this identity comes from without, rather than within. It is confined within our human birth, and it will die when we breathe our last breath. It is informed and directed only by the situations and events that are outside of us. It certainly isn't the truth of our Being. It is like our body is a cloak we wear to engage in this earthly existence. But the belief in separation—separation from God, from each other, from our good, from love or joy or health or well-being—is *not necessary* and is very detrimental to our ultimate experience of this wonderful life we live. In other words, we can either be in our body, use our beautiful mind, and be fully connected to Spirit and live enlightened, or we can live as a separate and finite being that will die. We feel small and lost and unfulfilled, and we feel disconnected from God, from Source, and from others.

The ego believes it is needed to bolster our body identity and protect us from harm. But our integrated spirit, mind, and body is all we need for identity, protection, freedom, and peace in this world.

To protect us, the ego is constantly judging things in our environment and labeling them as safe or not safe, same or different, good or bad, right or wrong. Our mind is constantly perceiving through the five senses and labeling, conceptualizing, categorizing, and generalizing all the images, sights, sounds, and smells into the thoughts that fill our mind.

Our minds do not even comprehend all that is going on around us. Through our senses, we take in a minimal amount of information and then categorize that data to keep the mind from being completely overwhelmed.

"As long as the ego runs your life, most of your thoughts, emotions, and actions arise from desire and fear."

—ECKHART TOLLE

The mind perceives, and can take in information without judgment. We can just stick with the facts, if we have trained ourselves to integrate spirit, mind, and body. But the ego is the belief that we are separate because it can *only* perceive with the five senses and it can only perceive that we are separate, different, and not connected to others. The ego doesn't intuit, doesn't feel with the heart, doesn't listen to that small still voice. It has its identification as a separate entity, not connected to anyone or anything, and its job is to protect and uphold this identity at all costs. The costs can be quite high.

Many of us have turned the ideas that we can identify ourselves as different, separate, and apart from others and that we can identify things or situations that may harm us into the idea that we *are not connected* at all to others, or to Spirit itself, and that life is *almost* always hurtful, harsh, and threatening. To make matters more complicated—the ego constantly drags us to live in the past with shame, guilt, or regret, or it projects fear, worry, or anxiety into the future based on its collection of past information (memories).

Yikes! Because of its fragility, the ego has an intense need to fortify itself. It compares itself with other people and wants to be more important, to have more things and prestige, to be recognized for how exceptional it is, because it is always aware that it is small and weak and separate. That is the ego's job description.

Our individualized mind, a localization of One Mind, is necessary and helpful while we are in our unique human form. It is very practical in the 3D world of effects. The mind remembers how to ride a bike, set the stove, or speak a language. It remembers our grandmother's favorite recipe for chicken and rice. It is the mind that lets us graduate from elementary school or medical school. And it is the mind, or thinking, that can protect the human body from harmful situations. The mind sets off alarms in our head if there is a snake in our path or the weather turns suddenly. The mind may judge someone we meet as dangerous or menacing. The mind often informs us based on outer circumstances and its collection of information and memories. The mind is a wonderful and unique connection to Spirit, to each other, and to the world around us. But we lose our ability to stay grounded in Spirit when the ego, the belief in separation, takes over.

The ego is always acting out of a desire for something it considers would make us better than someone else, or it is acting out of fear to protect us against someone else or to protect us from life. You may have noticed, the ego is incessantly chatty. There is that committee of voices in our heads that always has a running commentary on each and every thing we are doing, saying, or experiencing. The ego is like a group of very protective and gossipy family members with lots and lots of opinions. It is always voicing them! Do you have this committee of voices in your head? Can you recognize the very distinct personalities: the inner critic, the cheerleader, the nag, Dudley Do-Right, the wounded child. Ego thoughts are rampant until we train ourselves to balance our inner Self with mind and body. When we become aware of ego thoughts and the personalities, we can simply watch them, discern their value, or ask them to be quiet.

When we are connected to our spiritual Self—the consciousness that is aware of the voices—we allow the mind to do its job of informing us about the external world of circumstances, and we are not driven or controlled by false thoughts of separation.

"The ego, however, is not who you really are.
The ego is your self image; it is your social mask;
it is the role you are playing. Your social mask thrives
on approval. It wants control, and it is sustained
by power, because it lives in fear."

—DEEPAK CHOPRA

We decide to step out of fear and instead we are lifted into peace, love, and joy, even while we are informed by the perceptions of our finite mind. When thoughts of separation, fear, or lack enter our mind, we look at them, discern their value, and let them go. We can integrate spirit, mind, and body and let go of those thoughts which no longer serve us. We rest in our *whole* Self, and let go of the beliefs in a separate and finite self.

For many of us the ego-mind is the filter through which we most often see the external world. As such, the world appears lonely, limited, violent, and cruel. God-Mind on the other hand, is unlimited, unbounded, and unrestricted, and we have the ability to see and experience life through this integrated mind. Which one sounds more fulfilling to you?

Our Whole Self—Our Whole Life

Thinking constantly from the ego-mind limits us; we get in the habit of living life from the outside in, and we live from a very small piece of ourselves. We are so busy living our egoic life that we forget to live our *whole* life.

By releasing the monopoly our ego identity has over us, we wake up. We realize the truth of our Being, our spiritual Self, our unlimited Mind. We connect easily to our natural state of creativity and peace—and we live enlightened. When we are "awake," we feel more alive than when we are living in our ego.

The ego keeps us trapped in repetitive thinking without new, creative ideas or ways of expression. A sunset is just another time of day. The person serving my food is just another way to get my meal on time. But when we experience being awake, a sunset is unspeakably amazing, indescribably brilliant, and an absolute miracle in which we take part. The person bringing us food becomes like a friend on a mission to serve us, to help us, to participate in a beautiful moment in our day. We suddenly become awake to endless possibilities and to a definite sense of connection with all things and everyone. The present moment is alive and unlimited!

We can work hard on each and every negative or limiting thought and belief we have to neutralize its effect in our life. We can work diligently on overcoming our limiting thoughts about relationships, marriage, or how difficult it is to raise children as a single parent. We can work hard to neutralize our limiting beliefs on our health, our weight, or how unhealthy foods are today. We can work hard on neutralizing our negative beliefs on how tough it is to find a job that perfectly expresses who we are or to find work that will make us a million dollars in a crashing economy. We can work hard on uncovering and replacing our limiting beliefs about money, about how difficult it is to get, to make, to keep, or about the national debt or world pandemic situations. We can work hard and overcome anything through workshops, retreats, affirmations, journaling, therapy, practices, prayer.

OR we can transcend our limiting thoughts, our ego-identity, our habits, and our current situations and enter the enlightened awareness, our natural state of Oneness and Wholeness. It is "closer to us than our breathing, nearer to us than our hands and feet." It is not a great leap to get there, because *there* is right here. It is who and what we are. When we integrate Spirit with mind and body, we sustain enlightened living and we don't have to dissect every old thought or feeling. Instead, we align with our God-Self, our Wholeness, and we are guided and directed to our highest good, always. It is right where we are all the time.

Balancing the Inner and Outer Voices

The mind and thinking do not disappear. They will always be a part of us as long as we are in human form. But as a human being, we don't need the thoughts or beliefs in a *separate self*; those beliefs are so very destructive. It's necessary to challenge our thoughts, our beliefs, and the committee of voices in our head in order to fully integrate spirit, mind, and body.

One of the best ways to recognize our ego-identity is to become aware of our thoughts, to watch them as they come and go and use discernment before entertaining them. I have learned to be good friends with my thinking. I treat my ego like a child, because it is like a child with its limited information and resources. When my ego is talking incessantly, I just ask it to be quiet. When it judges someone as a potential threat, I thank my ego, like I would a well-meaning (but small-minded) friend. I assess the situation from my whole perspective, my enlightened Self, and choose how I want to respond. I can always take into consideration the information my ego provides, but I make decisions from my integrated Self, the whole of my Being. When the ego voice begins to gossip or criticize, I thank it for doing its job, and I choose to see the beauty and uniqueness within myself and in every single person. My ego is a part of me, like my hands and eyes, but with its limited perspective, it shouldn't be running the show!

When we allow our powerful integrated Self to radiate throughout our lives, the ego-identity recedes. When we are in our enlightened state of consciousness, we are at peace or in harmony with what is. We become acutely aware of the ego talk of the committee, we engage where we need to engage, and we release everything else. We see events and situations from a unique and integrated perspective.

There are ways to become more and more aware in our everyday life, simple ways of feeling awake and alive and present in every moment, of experiencing the peace that passes human understanding in the small daily tasks that take up most of our everyday existence. Turning within through meditation and mindfulness connects us to the Eternal Presence, slows our ego-mind down to a murmur, and allows us to experience the awe and wonder of our true nature and the nature of the Universe. The love and joy that comes to us naturally, for no apparent reason, is always right here waiting to explode from within us and pour itself out into everything we do and say and into every situation. It is right where we are always, in the present moment, now.

Sometimes we may need to train ourselves with spiritual practices to transcend our perceived limitations, the ego version of who we are, and to realize the Eternal Essence of who we are as All-Mighty, Unlimited, Unbounded Creativity, and Unconditional Love. And sometimes, in a moment, or a breath, we experience the Peace that passes all understanding. Why is it called "Peace that passes all understanding?" Because it isn't egoic; it isn't a peace that comes from the situations and events in our life. It is a peace that emanates from the Presence within. This peace is never determined or diminished by circumstances. The ego cannot give us peace; at best, it can offer only a temporary calm in the storm of its chatter. True Peace comes from within, from our connection to it.

CHAPTER 5

An Integrated Life

When we are not aware of our Infinite Nature, we feel separated from Source and wander around in this world of effects, living life from the tip of the iceberg. We live from the outside in. When we live from the limited world of effects, we believe we are victims of circumstance, that ultimately we are victims of our upbringing, our parents, our education, our society, our past, our mistakes, the limitations of our body, our health, etc. Some of us feel blessed that at least we were victims of good circumstances, but even then, we walk through life feeling small and helpless, not feeling that the world really works for us, that we are lucky just to get by. At best, we feel lucky; at worst, we feel subjected to a harsh world and an unhappy life.

There is a depth and breadth to life, and unlimited possibilities available to us, if we could only see through the veil and take the time and energy to connect with our Spiritual Self.

Jesus taught, "I and my Father are one." All the wisdom traditions teach this one profound truth, that Spirit created us in its image and likeness and that we are not the small, frail, limited humans that we appear to be from the outside. Instead, we are unlimited, powerful, loving, and creative beings.

"We take that which is unreal to be real and that which is real to be unreal."

—RUPERT SPIRA

So, how can we, as individuals, stand in the truth of Wholeness and live fully in our lives, relationships, jobs, and circumstances? When we embrace completely these universal principles that we read about in this book, we experience for ourselves, unequivocally, a world that works *for* us. How does it serve the world if I cannot free myself of my own false identity? If I am a prisoner in my own ego? How can I change the world out there when I struggle to change the events in my own life? When I come to realize that it is done to me as I believe, and I am experiencing lack, I learn to take responsibility to change my thoughts, change my beliefs, change my stories, change my perspective. I take responsibility to change so I then experience a world of abundance, a world that works for me, a world in which I fulfill my divine purpose. To do this I learn to integrate spirit, mind, and body.

We cannot, in any real or lasting way, accept for others what we cannot accept for ourselves. I cannot sit here and write about living enlightened and co-creating the effects in my world unless I have practiced these principles and practices, experimented with them, and proven it to myself with significance and success. We cannot give to others what we don't have. When we turn within, we are able to recognize all that we are, all that we have, and all that we are able to do and to give.

According to the Gospel of Thomas, Jesus said, "If you bring forth what is within you, what you bring forth will save you. If you do not bring forth what is within you, what you do not bring forth will destroy you." He was talking about this intense and powerful Presence that lies within each of us. It moves us, breathes us, and has Its being as us. It is the truth of who we are. And if we bring it forth, if we allow it entrance into our life by living in Presence and putting the ego in its rightful place, it will save us. It will save each of us from poverty, addiction, suffering, and loneliness. However, if we do not bring it forth, if we do not allow the inner wisdom of Wholeness and Oneness that we possess within to come forth, the lack and limitation of living only from the ego-mind will crush us, crush our true identity, our joie de vivre.

"Power that is released and circulated flourishes and grows. Power confined stagnates and destroys."

—CHRIS MICHAELS

We unknowingly create barriers and obstacles in our lives; we repeat unhealthy patterns over and over, and nothing we accomplish on our own will bring true satisfaction. Inevitably, if we continue to persist in ignoring the power within each of us, it will turn inward on itself and destroy the outlet it created for its own expression: our human self. And we suffer in stress and unhappiness.

With practice, we fully embrace this life we are given with the understanding that we are co-creators and that when we create from the place of absolute love, with our desire, with our integration and acceptance, then we experience a world that works for us. As a co-creator, it is vital that you not just read about the practices that are present here, but actually *do* them. We will easily be able to imagine with these spiritual practices, as they are represented by all the mystical traditions around the globe, a world that works for each of us, our family, our community, and the world. It begins with us!

Spiritual practices are the path that leads to *experiencing* our enlightenment. These practices allow us to access more easily the state of consciousness that is the kingdom of Heaven. Just like an athlete spends hours each day, every week, month after month, to prepare for the moments she will test her body in competition, so too we practice day after day so that we are fully prepared to live our authentic life, to live a joyful life, a life of health, prosperity, and love, especially when situations arise that seem challenging.

If we cannot access the state of consciousness in which we feel Oneness when we are still and comfortable, how will we access that state when we are busy, bothered, or severely disturbed by our surroundings? When we receive an unexpected diagnosis? When the stock market hits an all-time low? When we are proficient at living enlightened, these spiritual activities are no longer practices; they become our integrated way of being in the world.

When we *experience* Spirit flowing in and throughout our life, living us, breathing us, we live our purposeful life from our whole being; we live as a human and spiritual Being, a fully integrated human Being.

The present moment, right here and now, is the only point of power, the point of integrating the human and the divine. The following chapters are a guide to letting go of what is in the way of being present in the moment that is presenting itself right now. I invite you to step into a new and fully integrated way of living and being. When we live enlightened, we can feel the depth and breadth and totality of that infinite iceberg underneath us, supporting us, connecting us to all of our Good.

Section 2

Letting Go—
Deconstructing
Old Beliefs

We are meant to be brilliant,
creative, unlimited Beings.
When you tire of being the caterpillar,
become the butterfly!

CHAPTER 6

Letting Go and Resting in Truth

For most of us, there is a process of letting go of the cocoon that we have wrapped around ourselves. It is the comforting cocoon of old beliefs, outdated rituals, and an outmoded worldview of the way things work. To live enlightened, we never need to add one iota to ourselves. We are whole, perfect and complete. But we may need to spend some time in letting go of the false self.

Begin in the Beginning

Remember those moments of feeling complete Oneness? It's as if you are connected to something so much bigger than yourself; you feel expansive, powerful, and completely supported. When we know that enlightenment is an experience of Oneness, of Wholeness, we begin at the beginning and we clarify what we are One with, Whole in. The answer is we are one with All There Is, Was, and Ever Will Be, the Allness, Wholeness, and Fullness and No-thing-ness of Life, but that is an incredibly long title. In many religious traditions, there is a name for this All, such as God, Allah, Brahman, Elohim. But what is God?

The first words of the Tao Te Ching state, "The tao that can be told (named, talked about) is not the eternal Tao." It means that the god that can be named is not the eternal God. This is true because once we name something, we've given it a symbol. The symbol stands for what we have named, but the symbol is not what we have named, just as a statue or a painting of God is not actually God and doesn't represent or express all that God is. The statue or painting is only one small, finite, and limited idea about God. It is the idea of the infinite nature of Spirit compressed into a shape, size, color, image. In that shape or form, it no longer represents All. When we use words to label, which we must do to communicate externally with others, we often forget the "whole" behind the word and the word loses its potency and meaning.

"In one drop of water are found all the secrets of all the oceans; in one aspect of you are found all the aspects of existence."

−KAHLIL GIBRAN

If someone has never been to the ocean, we might use certain words to describe the ocean to them. We could draw pictures of the ocean we've seen, but that would only be one very small representation of the vast aspects and differences in all the oceans. We could say the ocean is blue, or blue-green, or gray depending on the ocean we know. We could describe the saltiness, or sandiness, or rockiness, or the wind, shells, or waves that are often at the ocean. But everything we could say or do would only describe a limited aspect of the ocean and certainly not present an actual experience of what the ocean is.

If you have been to the ocean, you have had a visceral experience of it and it is alive within you. You can close your eyes and connect to that experience, feel the wind on your cheek, smell the salt in the air, hear the crashing of the waves and the sounds of the gulls. There isn't really one word that contains the whole of this experience. And that is only one experience of one ocean in one moment. Similarly, there isn't one word that defines the experience of knowing what this thing called God is.

While it may not be possible for every person on the planet to experience the ocean, it is entirely possible that every person could experience or know the Unlimited Creative Source that many call God, Creator, or Infinite Intelligence. It is who and what we are, our very essence. It is within, and it is right now.

The definition of this Unified Field of Creativity is very hard to clarify and almost impossible to agree on. Gary Zukav said, "I don't have a definition of God, because I've never really understood that word. People have different understandings of it and it's caused a great deal of conflict. If I had to say what would my definition of God be, if I were going to use that word, I would say that this universe has layers upon layers upon layers of compassion and wisdom beyond ours." Debbie Ford said, "I define God as an energy. A spiritual energy. It has no denomination, it has no judgment, it has an energy that when we're connected to it we know why we're here and what we're here to do." That is describing the enlightened connection. "God is an all-encompassing love that is the source of all, the reality of all, and the being through which I am," states Marianne Williamson. Albert Einstein said, "That deeply emotional conviction of the presence of a superior reasoning power, which is revealed in the incomprehensible universe, forms my idea of God." And Deepak Chopra believes, "God is the evolutionary impulse of the universe. God is infinite creativity, infinite love, infinite compassion, infinite caring." One of my favorite insights comes from Eric Butterworth: "God is not loving, God is the allness of love. God is not wise, God is the allness of wisdom. God is not a dispenser of divine substance, God is the allness of ever-present substance in which we live, move, and have being. God is not a being."

God is One. There is only One Life and everything participates in it. There is only One Mind and everything participates in it. There is only One Beingness and it lives, moves, and expresses as all beings. We are not finite beings resting in an Infinite Beingness; we are Infinite Beingness resting in a finite being. When we live this, we live an integrated life.

"To become learned, each day add something.
To become enlightened, each day drop something."

—LAO TZU

The first practice in becoming enlightened is to let go of the limited ideas we have created for the Eternal Essence of all life and allow it to be All That It Is. As we dive into undoing our limited concepts of this Ultimate Reality, we come to understand Spirit not as an anthropomorphic man or woman, or a being or an entity, or a state of consciousness, or something to be found or gotten, but as Life, as seen and unseen, energy and movement, music and language, birth and death, All-There-Is-and-More.

We constantly come in contact with Infinite Source as we sink into the silence of conscious awareness and re-establish the ever-present connection with the One Mind that is God. We then have the experience of the indwelling Spirit, and the universal presence of Life. Without words and concepts, with just *experience,* we intuitively sense and know the All as all, and we know the All as who and what we are.

God is All There Is, Was, and Ever Will Be. God is every-thing, and no-thing, visible and invisible, imaginable and the unimagined as yet. Many of us experience this often throughout the day without even realizing it! It is a moment in between thoughts or breath. You can experience this right now. Close your eyes and ask yourself: what is my next thought? Pause… in the space it takes to turn your attention inward, there is a moment of spacious awareness, of alertness, and that is the unlimited Mind of Spirit which holds infinite possibilities. Similarly, you can ask yourself: "Am I aware?" In looking for the answer, the mind pauses. Where does the attention go? When we let go of what we are aware *of,* we become aware of being aware; that is the still, silent presence of God. It is that moment between the thought and breath.

It is not complicated but simple. It is not exotic but natural. It is so simple in fact, that we often overlook this most natural connection to Source.

First Impressions of God

One of the most exciting things about living enlightened every day is that our concept of Spirit, the Eternal Essence, continually expands. I grew up in the Catholic church, where there were very definitive impressions I created about God and Heaven, mostly a man with a flowing white beard who was sometimes loving and gentle, sometimes angry and vengeful, but very human in my childlike mind. What were some of your earliest ideas around God? Were they comforting or a bit frightening?

It's funny how we hold on to such early influences in our lives. Through my years of spiritual practice, I came to understand Infinite Source in a much bigger way. The Love Intelligence that creates and governs the Universe is so much more than the sun and the sky and the galaxies, and so much more than human.

"Truth is One, the sages speak of it by many names."

—THE VEDAS

In the beginning is God and only God. There is nothing opposite of it, nothing other than it. Just Presence. In current scientific terms, we could say that before the big bang, there was the All and only the All. It follows then that after the big bang occurred, there was still only the All.

Before the big bang, this All existed as no-thing; no things existed, just Presence as Infinite Possibilities, the unseen and unmanifested.

After the big bang, there is still only the All but now as both the seen and unseen, the known and the unknown, the forms and the formless. The All is Infinite Possibility. All possibilities of anything and everything exist in and as the Divine Creator.

The All is also all finite forms, all manifestation of form, including thoughts, creativity, wisdom, etc. The Creator creates all of creation and is the way all creation is manifested.

The All There Is is so much bigger than I can hold in my heart or my mind. And yet *how* the All shows up in my life—as the faces of the beautiful people I meet, the ever changing dusk and dawn, the miracle of a newborn life, the smiles and wrinkles of the old people, the flowers and squirrels in my garden, my beloved son's beaming face, the peace that overcomes me and connects me to Its core—is so concrete and apparent.

When we remember that the Lord our God is One, then we understand that there is only One life, One activity, One presence that is always expressing and unfolding everywhere—and it is us, each of us. We—all of humanity—are God's presence on the planet!

God is Universal and Personal

It is not enough to imagine that Universal Presence is up there, out there, over there. We must include and know that Spirit is also who and what we are. The All is both personal and universal. Spirit is both within and without.

"God is beyond all the forms of life, but also
indwells every form of life as their essence.
God is both beyond and within."

—ECKHART TOLLE

Nothing comes to us unless it comes through us, through
our willingness to recognize it and accept it. Abundance,
prosperity, relationships, fulfillment, health, wealth, and well-
being don't come to us from a source *out there*. Spirit whispered our name, created us in its Nature. We are the eternal
emanations of the Divine. God is both transcendent and
immanent. It transcends all of creation. It is bigger than all
of its creation, and it is also imminent, present right here and
now, alive, within all of creation. God as One is also God as
All. God within is also God without. God is all of Life, in all
Life, and the life of all.

"You know that there is something more. There is a
power and a presence in the universe which responds
to us so completely, so perfectly, that we shall be
amazed when we understand the truth."

—DR. WILLIAM HORNADAY

Take a Moment: Remember How You Came to Know God

As we move into an enlightened understanding of Wholeness, it's important to use some self-inquiry to help us identify how we think about and experience Spirit, Source, or God in our life.

I invite you to get comfortable, grab a journal, and sit for a few minutes, relaxing and focusing on your breath. Then gently ask yourself these questions. Once you have pondered your thoughts, write them down slowly so you fully understand how these moments and experiences have affected your life.

▶ What are your earliest memories of God, Allah, YHWH, Brahman, or any other word you used or use for the Absolute? What did you understand? What was confusing? What was comforting?

▶ Did others around you have different ideas about, or different names for God?

▶ What are your most significant experiences of the presence of God in your life?

▶ What limiting beliefs are you willing to change or let go of in order to move into a more complete experience of Source?

CHAPTER 7

Creation, Creating, the Created

Have you ever wondered how the Universe creates? Modern science can't explain creation or consciousness, or many other universal ideas and concepts. It's interesting that most mystical traditions have a very similar version of the creation process, a universal cosmology. Those who have experienced enlightenment recognize this process and allow it to flow in their everyday lives.

If we imagine the All There Is before any "thing," i.e. before the big bang, we can imagine this Self-Existent Creator imagining, thinking inside itself, desiring expression, and then exploding into creation, the big bang of exhibition and manifested form. And the universe is continually being formed, continually expanding, continually expressing. Spirit thinks into itself; and through a very precise Law of itself, what it imagines, it forms, manifests, and makes real as itself. We can recognize this as three steps or stages in the Creative Process of Spirit, often symbolized as the triune nature of Life represented in many religions. When we think of Spirit as Infinite Possibilities, Infinite Creativity, the Unmanifested, the Invisible; in Christianity, we would call this God the Father.

The manner through which Spirit manifests itself is the Great Law. This Law is accepting and impersonal. It can only create what Spirit holds in Mind for it to create. It creates water, lightning, electricity, earth. It absolutely must create what it holds as a consistent idea. It is an impersonal Creative Law, or Medium. In Christianity, we could think of this as the Holy Spirit, the holy Law—the means through which the Infinite creates.

And the myriad forms of Creation are the manifest body of the All. They are everything proceeding from the big bang. Every. Single. Thing. We would compare the manifested forms of God, God's creations, to the Body of God, or in Christian terms, the Son of God.

"God is always begetting Its only begotten."

—MEISTER ECKHART

The Creative Process

We know a seed holds within it all the information it needs to become the thing which it is intended. It's incredible: A seed is a complete blueprint for what will become its form! An orange seed contains within it the information to become an orange tree and no other kind of tree. An acorn will always produce an oak, and a watermelon seed will never produce a strawberry. When we desire for something to grow, we place that specific seed into the soil. We know soil as a medium for growing plants, trees, vegetables, etc... That's why one of the easiest ways to explain and explore the creative process of Spirit is to use a gardening metaphor—the seed, the soil, and the plant.

"The garden is a metaphor for life, and gardening is a symbol of the spiritual path."

—LARRY DOSSEY

There is an invisible process, a hidden law, that takes place when we place a seed into a healthy soil in which the seed transforms, sprouts, and grows. In time, the sprout reaches through the topsoil, the appropriate plant is visible, and the fruits, flowers, or vegetables flourish.

"The creation of a thousand forests is in one acorn."

—RALPH WALDO EMERSON

The Seed, the Thought, the Beginning

When Spirit holds a thought, an idea within itself, the thought contains everything it needs to come into fruition, or to sprout into the world of form. In quantum theory (simplified), there are infinite possibilities, and making a specific choice collapses all the possibilities into just one, the one contained in that particular thought or seed. Spirit has a thought and moves from Infinite Possibilities to a particular event. Held within this thought is everything the event needs to come into full fruition, the blueprint. The thought itself is a complete event, even though it has not yet manifested in form, and like a seed, everything is poised and ready to spring forth from it.

The Soil, the Creative Medium, the Law

It is helpful for our human mind to imagine a way, a manner in which thoughts or ideas come into form.

"All is Love, yet All is Law."

—ERNEST HOLMES

This way is the Law of Mind. It is a law, just like our natural laws of gravity and aerodynamics. It is a law in that it cannot change, there are no exceptions, and it works the same every time. A law is unchanging. This Law of Spirit must produce whatever is planted into it, or held in Mind. The Law can only receive, say yes, and then manifest or produce any seed or thought put into it.

The Law does not judge whether the thought is good or bad, right or wrong, in the same way that gravity does not work only for something right and not for something wrong. The Law doesn't determine what is in the seed; that is already determined by choosing the thought or word. The Law only receives, nurtures, and grows the thought or seed into fruition. The divine Ideas of Spirit flow into its own divine Medium, or Law, and then make themselves visible, or manifest, as the Body of God, all of creation.

The Plant, the Body, the Visible Stuff

Everything visible was first created in Mind. The All, as No-Thing-ness, desires expression, and everything proceeds from this desire. Spirit speaks or thinks, or urges unto itself and through itself and within itself, and creates itself in form.

All forms, everything we can see in the world, is an effect. It was first created as an idea and then made manifest in form. It is helpful to think of the world of effects, or the world of form, as the secondary creation, with the first creation being the thought in the Mind of Spirit.

Everything in the world of form was an idea first, a choice, a desire. Everything in the world of form will shift, change, grow, and die. Everything in the world of effects will pass. Everything in the world of form is a temporary expression of the Divine. Nothing in the world of effects changes the Nature of the All.

The Word

In the Christian New Testament, John 1:1 states, "In the beginning was the Word." This could also be translated as, "Before the beginning, God." And then the *word* of God creates the beginning, the big bang of manifestation. John 1:2 continues, "and the Word was with God and the Word was God." What does that mean?

In the beginning, before anything, comes an original idea, a seed or blueprint. As the idea formulates, there comes the desire for expression, then the word, a symbol of the thought or desire. The word is with God, within God, is transmuted by the Law of God, and passes into the Form of God, which is also God! The Word, thought, or idea was before anything and then, through Law, became everything. The word creates All There Is in form. There is nothing other than the Oneness and Wholeness of Spirit, regardless of the myriad of forms, people, or galaxies. It is the Oneness of Spirit expressing.

John said that, "Out of the Word all things were made and without the Word was nothing made." The word, or thought, is the creative power of Spirit. The Law of Spirit obeys the word, and the forms of Spirit are in alignment with Itself. Spirit is the animating force of Its forms.

Take a Moment: Imagine the Creative Process

Can you imagine the creative process at work? This is one of the most practical and important concepts to understand and realize on the path of living enlightened. Take some time in a quiet place and just imagine Spirit as the Great Gardener!

▸ Visualize God as Infinite Possibilities, slumbering in No-Thing-ness. All possibilities exist, but no contrast, no form, no concepts. Imagine how this All might desire to experience Itself as color and sound, time and space, as infinite forms of beingness, activity, and sensation.

▸ Now imagine the big bang as an expression of Infinite Possibility passing into finite form. In your mind's eye, imagine looking at the earth and the sea, the stars, the sun, the moon, the creatures all around you. See them as part of the ever-expanding conscious creation of Spirit. In your imagination, can you see the earth forming, like a flower unfolding in the garden?

▸ Everything you see, everything you can imagine, everything that exists, flows from this One Source, including you! Feel, sense, and know YOU are created from the conscious creation of Infinite Mind. Can you feel yourself as an extension of the one Life of Source?

▸ Can you imagine the process, or Law, that exists within the One for It to be able to manifest All There Is? Just like the law of gravity, the Law of Spirit is always saying yes to the seeds, the ideas placed into it. Remember, this law, like all other laws, is impersonal. It can only receive and say yes; it can only nurture what has been placed into it. It can't decide what is worthy, right, or good.

▸ Take some time to write in your journal any images or thoughts that come from this process.

CHAPTER 8

As Above, So Below

Spirit created us, all of humanity, in its image and likeness. "Image and likeness" means "in the same nature, or in the same manner." We inherited the very nature of the One Creator, which means as Spirit creates, so too in that same manner, we create. The microcosm reflects the nature of the macrocosm; humanity reflects the nature of Divinity.

> "As above, so below, as within, so without,
> as the universe, so the soul"
>
> —HERMES TRISMEGISTUS

Created in the Image and Likeness of Spirit

We have the same nature or character as Spirit. It created us in Its image and likeness, not the other way around. We have been creating images and likenesses of a deity that is a like a man: sometimes angry and dissatisfied, limited, jealous, tempestuous, and the ultimate puppet-master, with us as the puppets. We have been creating this image for thousands of years. And yet, the opposite is true. Think about it. The Creator made us in Its Image, and every single human has a different image. Not one face is the same. Not one body, one color, one shade. Not even one fingerprint is the same. Not one strand of hair. And in nature, not one tree, leaf, blade of grass, or grain of sand is the same. That means Creation is and loves diversity and individuality. The creative Eternal Essence of absolutely everything creates everything utterly unique!

Even more astounding, the Creator made us in Its likeness or nature, which means we are *like* the Creator. As the Eternal Essence creates everything different, so too do we. We create with the same Creative Process described above. We create our situations, our circumstances, our relationships, and we create them differently than any other human ever has and ever will. The Eternal Essence will never happen again like you or like me, so we must find the fullest embodiment of who we are as the Divine Expression right here and now.

"We're fields of energy in an infinite energy field."

—E.E. CUMMINGS

How do we come to know intimately that we create as the Eternal Essence? We turn within and we seek to know ourselves, and we find God. We speak our word in alignment with our true Nature and we witness the results. We use our words to create the changes we wish to see in our life. We experience ourselves as co-creators with Source, and through the Law, we experience the results of our thinking.

Life doesn't just happen to us; we are not victims of circumstance—we participate and co-create our life experiences with our words, thoughts, and feelings. When we think, feel, and live in a place of Peace and Love and Joy, we create even more situations of peace and love and joy in our life. When we recognize the Truth of our being, we revel in life because we are resting in the kingdom of Heaven.

The Seeds, the Thought, the Results

We are always experiencing the results of the past seeds we have planted. Our thoughts are things, and when backed with feeling and emotion, they are extremely powerful. Our thoughts, backed with feeling and emotion, which we think consistently and repetitively, are producing the myriad of scenarios in our lives.

"The words you speak become the house you live in."

—HAFIZ

For example, if I have the thought, "I am going to fail my final exam," that thought could just slip away into nothingness; or I address the thought and think, "I AM going to fail this test," and the ego starts running rampant: "I haven't studied enough. I am not smart enough. I don't do well on tests." This produces ill feelings, anxiety, and worry and changes my body chemistry. If I continue to think more and more often, "I am going to fail," and it is backed by the powerful emotions of worry and self-doubt, I am setting up circumstances to fail.

On the other hand, I could address the thought by reminding myself to turn within and rest in my true nature, the nature of Spirit. I would then feel surrounded by good, by God. From that space I can choose to think, "I have studied, I have prepared, I generally do well on tests, I am ready." I become relaxed. I choose the thought "I am ready," and that is backed by a relaxed feeling. Whichever scenario I choose to think regarding the outcome of the test, whether I believe I will do badly or that I will do well, I am right. The consistent thought I plant into the Law will produce a consistent result.

The Law can only produce what it is given. It is done to me as I believe. The important thing to note is that I choose. We have to become aware enough of our thoughts, our fears, and our doubts in order to change them. We have to remember to step out of the thinking and into the spaciousness of awareness.

The Soil, the Creative Medium, the Experience

We can't see the law of gravity, but we can definitely demonstrate its effect. We can't see the law of aerodynamics or the law of buoyancy, but we can experience their effects. If we make a boat out of a brick, it will sink because we did not use the law correctly. It's not the law that failed, but our understanding and use of the law that was flawed. We cannot see the law of cause and effect, but we can always see and experience its effects, and we can test our understanding of it.

"Scientific research can reduce superstition by encouraging people to think and to view things in terms of cause and effect."

—ALBERT EINSTEIN

We can witness and test laws. We might test the law of electricity in our house by hiring an electrician who installs the proper equipment in our home, the wires, switches, and receptors. We use the proper channels; we flip the switch and the light bulb comes on or it doesn't. If it doesn't, we know the law is absolute and it will absolutely work if we use it correctly. So we follow the wiring to see where we have not installed the equipment correctly; we fix it and go back to the switch, flip it, and the light comes on. The light turning on, or not, is our demonstration of whether we have used the law correctly. We can test our theory all day long. And just like the light bulb which doesn't turn on, when we are not seeing the situations, events, and circumstances we want and need in our lives, we can know the law is absolute. Therefore it is we who have a flawed or limited understanding of the law or who have used the law incorrectly.

Sometimes it is necessary to retrace our steps and see what thoughts or seeds we are putting into Law to be created. We discover the negative thoughts of lack or limitation which we are planting, and may have been planting for some time now. We can remove the weeds and replant powerful, positive beliefs.

"Cause and effect, means and end, seed and fruit,
cannot be severed; for the effect already
blooms in the cause, the end pre-exists
in the means, the fruit in the seed."

—RALPH WALDO EMERSON

The Creative Law that holds the sun, the moon, and the planets in place is the same Creative Law that becomes personal to each of us. It is a universal law and, consciously or unconsciously, we use this law to create the situations, events, and circumstances in our lives.

Other religions describe the law of cause and effect in different ways. In Hinduism, it is called Karma—the sum of a person's actions in this and previous states of existence, viewed as deciding their fate for future existences. It means that everything you give out will come back to you. Or put differently, you reap what you sow. Some would say the very foundation of Buddhism is Karma, the great law of cause and effect, which believes we are the result of all our past thoughts.

Moses saw the law of cause and effect as very exacting: an eye for an eye. It is an accurate description in the Universal sense; the Law must give back what we put into it. It is said the teacher Jesus came to fulfill the Law, not to destroy it. This means that Jesus taught us to personalize the Law, and to create from love and Wholeness, so that we may live wholly and in love. Knowing and believing in this Law and the creative process is key to creating a wonderful life. It never matters what has come before. The creative power is available right now, in this moment.

"Truly, I say to you, whoever says to this mountain, 'Be taken up and thrown into the sea,' and does not doubt in his heart, but believes that what he says will come to pass, it will be done for him. Therefore, I tell you, whatever you ask in prayer, believe that you have received it, and it will be yours."

—MARK 11:23–24

Most of us don't need a mountain to be displaced into the sea, but we might need a new job or to heal a relationship or an aspect of the physical body. When we sense and feel the love and the power of the Creative Energy within us, we can believe in receiving what we want.

When Jesus said, "I and my Father are one," He was asking us all to recognize and know our true and Divine heritage. When He said, "It is not I, but the Father, the Creator, who the does the work," He was referring to the Law. The Law transforms thoughts and feelings into form. Jesus also said these and greater things will you do, if you believe. Well, what do you believe? Jesus taught that we are all, every one of us, the sons and daughters of the Divine and that we have dominion over the world of effects, the world of form, and that we have dominion over our mind.

When we live from our ego-mind, we create with the ego thoughts, thoughts of separation, lack, and limitation. When we integrate with Spirit, we open ourselves up to an infinite world of possibilities, and we choose to turn those possibilities into the realities that fulfill us.

The Law is impersonal, always works, and can only say yes. It does not care about the results of its action; it has no conscience, no concept of good or bad, right or wrong, in the same way that electricity can light up a home or cause a deadly electric shock. A Law knows only to act upon what we place into it. The spacious sky cannot say no to the clouds which are formed. The clouds, no matter how dense, how ugly or unruly, can leave no mark or trace on the spacious sky. Spirit is like this. We can hold on to limiting, fearful thoughts or loving, joyful thoughts. We can believe the world is frightening or we can believe in goodness, and the law will say yes to it all.

The Plant, the Body, and the Body of Our Affairs

We are using free will to choose our thoughts, and thereby the direction of the Law's activity.

"We reap what we sow."

−GALATIANS 6:7

If we plant an orange seed, we will reap an orange tree and not an apple tree. If we plant rosemary, the soil cannot produce oregano, only the rosemary that we planted. When we sow the seeds of negativity and despair or lack and limitation, we can only reap what we sow. And when we sow consistent thoughts of peace, prosperity, and joy, we will reap those as well.

Everything in our lives is a creative activity of one form or another. Some people create good for themselves, others create despair. Most of us seem to haphazardly create a little of both. As we grow in knowledge and conviction and we become familiar with the way the Law works, we are more and more able to swing the creative activity of our thoughts to a favorable side.

It's not a matter of *when* you will manifest or *if* you will manifest; you already *are* manifesting, right now. Look around you. The life you are living is the life you created and continue to create. If you want to create something new in your life, create it in your mind, feel it in your heart and your awareness, and believe it is done. Jesus reminds us, "It is done to you as you believe." And, he reminded us, that it is done *within,* and it is done now.

"Child of God, you were created to create the good, the beautiful, and the holy."

—A COURSE IN MIRACLES

The Law of Attraction

The Law of Attraction simply stated is that like attracts like. Any object, which is energy, is always vibrating at a certain frequency which in turn attracts other objects, situations, circumstances, and opportunities similar in vibration. When we realize and maintain our highest frequency, we attract our highest and best good. Like all organic forms, our body is made up of elemental compounds with a frequency and magnetism. All is energy. We are energy and we are vibrating at a particular frequency, which travels up and down the frequency range, depending on how we are feeling and what we are holding in mind and in our emotional body.

Scientists can measure the frequency of thoughts and emotions and have concluded that each has a frequency: A negative thought has a lower frequency than a positive thought. When we walk in enlightenment, when we understand and feel a deep sense of connection with everything and everyone, the Universe says, "Yes she is connected, give her more experiences that make her feel more connected." When we are joyful, we attract many more experiences that bring us joy, and when we are peaceful, we attract peace. We attract WHAT WE ARE in this moment (not what we wish for). What and how we are being is what we are attracting. This is another way to explain the creation process. Ultimately, what we think consistently, backed by emotions, we plant into the soil, and create a vibration which attracts to us a similar result.

Spiritual teachers have said much on the law of attraction or the law of manifestation. For me, in my life, there is one very easy and very simple law of attraction command and it never fails. I learned that whenever I want something—a new car, a new job, a better relationship, a bigger house—there is one common denominator: I want these things because I believe these things will in some way make me happy. Even if I want something to provide a sense of security, that will bring me joy. If I want something that allows me more freedom, that too will bring me joy. When I finally boiled down everything I wanted into joy, then I realized joy was my nature; it is a quality of the Divine, and I can recognize and revel in joy as my own essence whenever I please. That is when my life really changed. A quick side note: Even though we use the words interchangeably, the spiritual difference between happiness or joy as an emotion or a spiritual quality is monumental.

Joy as the spiritual quality of Presence never depends on external conditions. It is who and what we are, and we can connect with it at any time, under any circumstances. Happiness that can be described as an emotion comes and goes depending on our judgment of a circumstance as either good or bad, right or wrong. When something we deem good happens, we are happy; when something we decide is not good happens, we are not happy.

Even when wonderful things happen to us—we get the job, or the girlfriend, win the prize—the happiness we feel is temporary. It wears off, and often we begin to make a new list of all the things we will need to make us happy.

When we realize that Joy, Peace, Abundance, or Love is the core of our very nature, we can call these forth from within; we can feel and sense them as us. We then attract more situations that bring us these feelings and we reap the benefits of living enlightened. True joy, peace, and abundance are never connected to circumstances and events; they are our very essence.

"Everything is energy and that's all there is to it. Match the frequency of the reality you want and you cannot help but get that reality. It can be no other way."

—ALBERT EINSTEIN

Ultimately, we attract to us what we *are*, our very vibration, not what we want. When we want something, we are usually acknowledging lack, that we don't have this thing, or that; we are in a state of wanting, and the Law responds by giving us more wanting. Think about something you have longed for in the past. Maybe sometime when you have acknowledged, "If I only had the (house, relationship, money, education) then I would be (successful, happy, rich, able to give back, etc.). Wishing, wanting, and longing are states of lack. The Law is absolute and continues to give us more lack. When we turn within and acknowledge our true nature, our enlightened state of consciousness, we want for nothing; from this place of abundance, even more is given to us. When we are peaceful, loving, and kind, we attract situations and events that are even more peaceful, more loving, and more kind.

3 Magic Words: I Am...

The Universe will grant your every wish when you use these magic words: I Am _____ (Fill in the blank). The word you insert will activate the statement. These are now powerful words, always creating. What are you creating? Well, what do you say most often about yourself? Are you kind in your words about yourself? Are you harsh? Sometimes we don't realize how critical we are of ourselves. We've become deaf to the voices in our head that criticize, belittle, or injure ourselves and others; those voices are activating the Law nonetheless. Just because we have tuned them out, does not mean they are not active. One of the biggest hurdles I see with so many people is learning to redirect the powerful statements that begin with I Am.

When we turn within to the Source of our being, and recognize the truth of who we are, it is easy to change the direction of that thinking. We remember: "I am powerful; I am beautiful; I am kind, loving, compassionate, creative, brilliant, and wise! I am capable, unique, inspiring, and funny." We plant the seeds of truth in our garden, and we watch ourselves flourish and thrive! We release the voices of the past that we have allowed to take up residence in our minds, and we grow, we transform, we rise! Becoming aware of our thoughts as they enter our mind is so powerful because in becoming aware, we can see clearly and release previous conditioning and habitual programming, the seeds of the past. We can easily discern what is true and what is false. We can create and enjoy love, peace, and joy.

Take a Moment: Explore How to Finish the Sentence, I Am . . .

▸ What are the words that you most often use to complete that sentence? Are they uplifting? Are they voices from the past that express lack and limitation? Do they represent who you are now or who you see yourself to be in the future?

▸ Now, think of what you want to create using these positive action words now:

I am _____.

▸ Write any answers and insights in a journal. Plant new seeds and watch your new garden flourish!

What is Growing in Your Garden?

Our consistent thoughts, backed by feelings, produce the situations, circumstances, and events in our lives. It is easy to see how the things we have thought over our lifetime have greatly influenced our choices, our actions, and habits. And it is just as powerful to imagine that right now, we can choose again a new thought, a powerful thought, act on it, grow it into a habit, and allow it to change the direction of our life.

Buddha, Lao Tzu, and other great mystics and spiritual teachers are credited with this saying:

"Watch your thoughts, they become your words;
Watch your words, they become your actions;
Watch your actions, they become your habits;
Watch your habits, they become your character;
Watch your character, it becomes your destiny."

We are living in the world we've created with our words, actions, and habits that early on formed the character or personality traits of who we are. And this, step by step, leads us to our destiny.

Choose Again—Choose Now

Individually, we didn't create the sun and the stars, but we create how we respond to them. We didn't create the weather but we choose how we respond to it. We may not have created the details of our birth, but we create how we respond to these details now. Our parents, our family, wealth or poverty, health or disease—in everything, we are taking part in the creative process. We have responded and continue to respond and react to the situations, events, and circumstances in our life and therefore we continue the creative process.

When we look at the creative process in reverse, we can look outward at the situations, relationships, and circumstances in our life and see what our beliefs are. Literally! We can see that we have been planting seeds of abundance or lack, of love and friendship or solitude, of peace and poise or chaos and confusion. We can tell just by looking at the events and relationships that show up. If we don't like what we see or what we are experiencing, we can choose again.

We can change the thoughts we hold consistently in Mind only if we become aware of them. We can choose thoughts of love, abundance, health, and well-being, and we can trust that the creative process will return new results just as quickly as we plant new seeds and cultivate new habits.

"Be careful what you water your dreams with. Water them with worry and fear, and you will produce weeds that choke the life from your dream. Water them with optimism and solutions, and you will cultivate success. Always be on the lookout for ways to turn a problem into an opportunity for success. Always be on the lookout for ways to nurture your dream."

—LAO TZU

There is only one Creative Intelligent Power and no matter what we call it, the Law moves into action by our words, thoughts, and feelings. Feel joy, beauty, and love today, in this moment now, and this Power will fill your life with joy, beauty, and love.

Take Another Moment: Remember What It Takes to Create Something Wonderful.

We create with our words, our thoughts, and our feelings. You've been doing it your whole life. This exercise asks you to remember how you've done this in the past

‣ Meditate for a moment on something positive you have created in your life: a relationship, job situation, buying your first home, graduating college. When have you had a powerful idea, the desire to express the idea, and then found the form of this expression coming to fruition in your life?

‣ Ask yourself, "What was the seed I planted into Law to produce this particular situation? What were the thoughts I cultivated to bring forth the situation I wanted to experience?"

‣ Write down the thoughts as they come to you and record the creative process as it has worked in your life.

‣ In that quiet still space, ask yourself, "What do I desire to create now? What seed must I cultivate to allow this to grow into form in my life?"

Remember to cultivate these thoughts. Take at least 15 minutes each day to visualize and sense what it feels like to have what you desire in your life, then let it go and let the Law do the work. Turn within and experience the unlimited Truth of your being. By doing so, you call this Truth into fruition.

CHAPTER 9

It's an Inside Job

L iving life from the inside, or "insight," out is a total revolution in thought, and it is the thought that will revolutionize the world. That's why it's so important to realize that we commune WITH Spirit first and foremost. Then, we commune AS Spirit.

"When it seems humanly impossible to do more in a difficult situation, surrender yourself to the inner silence and thereafter wait for a sign of obvious guidance or for a renewal of inner strength."

—PAUL BRUNTON

From the minute we are born, the adults around us tell us to watch out, to hold on, to be careful, to protect ourselves, because there's not enough, we're not enough, someone else is smarter, younger, better, older, richer, thinner. We sense and see that we are separate beings, and we feel disconnected from each other and from God's Infinite Being. What will happen when we learn that we are One in Spirit, as Spirit from the moment we are born? We are powerful creative beings, connected to All. We create with the power of our thought, and never need to compete. We were born to create. Our creative spirit began in *consciousness first!* We can change anything, heal anything, resolve anything, build and grow anything according to our nature. We will live joyful and creative lives!

In the early stages of living enlightened, turning within and away from the world of effects is the simplest way to experience the Truth of our Being, our Spiritual Nature. It is the beginning of integrating spirit, mind, and body. Jesus said that when we pray, we are to go into our closet; He was not talking about a literal or physical closet, He was talking about turning our attention inward, to that place of inner knowing, turning within to the kingdom of Heaven. Jesus often taught that the kingdom of Heaven is within us, right where we are, and it is at hand now, in this moment. It is a state of consciousness in which we are aware of our true identity, that we are the sons and daughters of Spirit itself.

The kingdom of Heaven, then, is the state of enlightenment. We turn within to remember who we are. We go to that still, quiet space in the center of our being that is one with the Divine so we may connect with and experience what is holy and whole and unique to us as divine beings.

Heaven is right here and now, every day, hiding in plain sight. I am not talking about some special state of mind or being. Most of us experience this inner peace many times a day. The moment that we relax our attention on all the stuff, the moment before the next thought, the moment of stillness before the meeting or before picking up the kids from school. It is an everyday moment filled with peace because it is without conflict or chaos. It is a moment filled with possibility because we have stopped trying to make something happen. It is a moment of love because we have stopped thinking about what is in the way of being loving.

Meditation is Who We Are, not What We Do

A meditative moment reveals our true nature. Meditation is the key to enlightenment and enlightened living. Just as a key is used to unlock a door, meditation is used to unlock the secret to living fully and completely whole; and by the way, it's not really a secret!

"To the mind that is still, the whole universe surrenders."

—LAO TZU

We never have to quiet the ego-mind and it will never really be quiet; that isn't its nature. It would be like trying to still a bunch of chattering monkeys. Instead, we just go inside to our closet and shut the door. In meditation, we move easily into the stillness of our consciousness, and experience our true nature. There, it is already perfectly still, wonderfully quiet. This is the magnificent, quiet space of Infinite Possibility and Unbounded Creativity. Meditation is the time and place for our omniscient, omnipotent, omnipresent spiritual being to communicate with our unique expression as a human being. Meditation gives our human body a time and place to connect with our spiritual Self. It is a literal integration of our spirit, mind, and body.

The more still we become, the more we can hear. When we seek first the kingdom of Heaven, this simple state, all else will be added. We turn our attention inward, away from the noise and confusion of the world of effects, the world that our senses are always trying to compartmentalize and categorize, and we rest in our enlightenment. It is already given, and always available. It is God's good pleasure to give us the kingdom; however, the only way to *experience* it is to go beyond the world of ego, beyond the world of form, to release for a moment the chatter of the ego, and to live and create from the Truth of our Being.

We change nothing about our true identity when we meditate. We always have been and always will be the divine emanation of Spirit. When we meditate, we turn our attention away from the transitional world of effects. The ego-mind becomes a background noise, like the refrigerator humming, and we sit in communion *with* Spirit. Meditation connects us with our spiritual identity; when we feel connected to something so much greater than our small selves, we experience solutions to life's problems and even healing in our body. We become more balanced as a spiritual Being having a human existence.

When I practice Presence and being aware throughout the day, I notice I am in a very positive mood, I am receptive to new ideas while I am at work or with others, and I choose situations and even food that is better for me. For a while these may be the subtle benefits of integrating our meditation experience. I also have experiences of being connected to the Great Source of love, wisdom, and power, and these are the life-changing effects of an integrated meditation practice. I don't always have insights and revelations *when* I meditate, but I always have them *because* I meditate.

"The more tranquil a man becomes, the greater is his success, his influence, his power for good."

–JAMES ALLEN

The number one complaint people tell me about their meditation is, "It's not working." I explain that if you started running as exercise, and you came back from your first run, out of breath, physically sore, tired, and basically in the same shape, same weight and lung capacity as when you started the run, would you say it's not working? And the second time you ran, same thing. And the third time, you were even more tired and achy, you might say again, "It's not working." But we all know that if you stick to a new workout regimen and get past the boredom and discomfort, you will eventually see results. The effects of meditation are very similar. You may not even notice when your life changes, but your life will change! There are instant revelations about so many wonderful things when we let go of the thinking mind and rest in Divine Mind. Revelation means to lay bare, to make clear. When we bring meditation into everything we do, the interconnectedness of all life becomes clear. The meaning behind all relationships becomes clear. The joy underneath all circumstances becomes clear. When you bring meditation into everything you do, you are living enlightened.

We are the children of God, we are enlightened already! So why do we not always feel that the kingdom of Heaven is at hand now? Why do we not always feel that state of consciousness that is enlightenment? Why doesn't our life reflect a life of Peace that passes human understanding? Of unsurpassed Joy? Of compassionate, uncompromising, and unconditional Love? Because we are trapped in the ego-mind, our continually thinking, judging, discerning, agreeable or disagreeable, small mind. Why do we not always experience the kingdom of Heaven now? Because we are not actually present, in our spiritual center, *now*.

"Always hold fast to the present. Every situation, indeed every moment, is of infinite value, for it is the representative of a whole eternity."

—JOHANN WOLFGANG VON GOETHE

When we live life from the outside in, we aren't really living; we are busy doing. When we live this way, it is an unfulfilled life. With our body, our senses, the only way we can know things is they are always separate from us, other than us. We can choose to focus on the content of our life, the forms, the circumstances, situations, and the events—all those things that are out there, apart from us. Or we can focus on our connection to Spirit, to Source. This inner connection will always put us in alignment with whatever seems outside of us; that which our senses perceive as separate from us.

When we live from the inside out, we are in alignment, integrating our spirit, mind, and body. When we are living from the outside in, we can only live as separate and apart from our Oneness. When we connect to Source first, it allows us to remember the truth of who we are so that we can connect to others as the emanations of Source also; we see and recognize the God in them. Suddenly, we are surrounded by the expression of Spirit everywhere we look, in everything we hear, and in everything we do.

We are, each of us, unique expressions of the same Source and only secondly and superficially are we separated by cultural, religious beliefs, and preferences.

Experiencing the Integrated Self

How do we experience turning within and knowing who and what we are? Our goal is not to escape the earth to experience a heaven of the future; instead, we are challenged to bring an awareness of the kingdom of Heaven into every activity of our lives, no matter who we are with or what we are doing. When we adopt practices like communing first *with* Spirit, we then commune and communicate *as* Spirit. When we practice being present in this moment, letting go of the past and the future, we become the expression of Life we were always meant to be.

"The soul always knows what it needs to do to heal itself. The problem is silencing the mind."

—CAROLINE MYSS

We stop, we turn within, we breathe; we let go of ego thoughts, each one as it comes, and we rest in Spirit. We withdraw our attention from the world of effects and we remember that it is an inside job. Source, Spirit, is within and we turn to it right now. Our challenge is to bring that sense of Oneness to our conscious awareness every day. Whatever we wish to know, to accomplish, to have, to heal, to reveal, it is within. It's always an inside job.

"You must live in the present, launch yourself on
every wave, find your eternity in each moment.
Fools stand on their island of opportunities and look
toward another land. There is no other land;
there is no other life but this."

—HENRY DAVID THOREAU

There is no other moment than this one. Most of us perceive our lives from the outside, and then we internalize what is happening out there; we take it in and we dissect it, analyze it. We try to make sense of it and fix it at the point of the problem. Have you ever exhausted yourself, running from problem to problem, just trying to put out all the little fires in your life? It will have you running on empty! By the time something exists in form, by the time we see the result made manifest as external conditions, the creative process for that situation or circumstance has passed.

When we want to change something in our world of affairs, we must change it from the *inside*, from our consciousness, our awareness, and our thoughts and feelings. We must first know ourselves as Spirit, then choose a new idea/ seed to put into Law/soil.

When we turn within and align ourselves with the Presence of God, we are guided and directed to choose something better, something more powerful, something more amazing.

Through the practice of calming our minds, we gain access to the Infinite Mind and we allow new and creative ideas to flow into our everyday activities and relationships. It's an inside job.

A Calm and Quiet Mind

There are many forms meditation can take in our daily practice and in our lives, from the obvious sitting with legs crossed, closing the eyes, and calming the small mind to active breathing methods which can be calming or invigorating. There are musical meditations with drum circles or chanting. There are movement meditations such as dance, tai chi, and qigong. Walking, running, swimming, or any activity which produces a natural rhythmic breathing are wonderful moving meditations. Yoga in all of its myriad forms has been a movement meditation for thousands of years. When we practice meditation, we allow the space for our conscious awareness to inform all of our activities, such as washing the dishes, running errands, and making appointments.

Anything we do with purpose and intention, including the laundry, becomes a meditation. It brings a sense of peace and calm to us like we've never known, and a deep sense of purpose to even the smallest activity. Brushing a child's hair, or walking the dog in the rain all can lead to sahaj samadhi, bliss and alignment with the All There Is.

When we turn within and experience our Eternal Self, we experience power, beauty, and creativity and we kickstart the creative process. That is how we connect to our highest Good and choose again. We begin again every day. Every moment is a new opportunity. Stepping into the silence allows for a complete communion with All There Is and fills us with energy and vitality, our actual Life Force is energized and revitalized through our connection. Still your mind, if only for a moment, and you will experience Peace. Calm your mind often, and you *are* Peace.

"You have a treasure within you that is infinitely greater than anything the world can offer"

—ECKHART TOLLE

Have you heard of the saying that you cannot solve a problem from the level of the problem? If we are recycling our thoughts, our actions, and the constant thoughts we tell ourselves, we will keep recreating the same problem. To solve any problem, from health to wealth to relationships to creativity and productivity, we need to step into a place where that problem doesn't exist: within! All the answers to all of life's problems are within us. From within, we are guided and directed to choose new thoughts, new words; we feel intensely and joyfully the possibility of manifesting this word, and we rest in this creative process. It's an inside job.

Be the Observer

Becoming a witness or observer to our ego-mind is one of the most important practices in living enlightened. When we observe the ego-mind—the chatter, the fear, the bodily sensations that arise in our everyday living—we are not judging, just watching.

When we observe, we become free from reacting and we leave space to choose, to change, to create, to be, or to act if we wish to. We stop being *victims* of our thoughts, and we become *witnesses* and then choosers of our thoughts and creators of our dreams. We step out of the habits of ego and step into the wholeness of conscious awareness.

We are not our thoughts. We are the consciousness that observes the thoughts.

We are not our feelings. We are the consciousness that experiences the feelings.

We are not our bodily sensations. We are the consciousness that is aware of the sensations in the body.

Thoughts, feelings, and sensations constantly come and go; they change. But that which is aware is never changing. It is infinite and eternal.

We are pure consciousness. Unlimited, unbounded, infinite in nature. Often, however, we are programmed to identify with the limitations of our body, of our thoughts, and of our feelings.

You are not your body. Take a look in the mirror. You'll notice that your body is not the same one you had when you were 3, or 13, or 30. It is easy to notice that we are not the same body. Each cell in our body changes and grows and dies daily, weekly, or monthly. Our body is not our essential or true nature. It is a temporary, finite phenomenon of our infinite expression.

You are not your thoughts. As each thought arises into your awareness, you'll notice it recedes. It's gone. Another one comes, and another. Sometimes there is a space between. What do the thoughts arise into? Where do they go? Who is it that is aware of our thoughts? Our thoughts are not our true or essential nature. They come and go. Most of the time the thoughts we have are not even true or factual! We are the consciousness that is aware of the thoughts.

You are not your feelings. Sometimes we really want to identify with the feelings that seem to overcome the body, feelings of joy or bliss, feelings of depression or guilt, and everything else in between. The joy that arises from winning a tennis match or landing an account will fade after the event is over. Sorrow that comes from ending a relationship will fade over time. These feelings rise up into our awareness and will fade away soon enough. What is it that is aware of the joy or the sorrow? It is our infinite Being, our unlimited consciousness, our God-Self.

We can imagine all of our thoughts and feelings and all of the sensations as clouds that come and go in the open, spacious sky that is our awareness. Just as the clouds never change the nature of the sky, never leave a trace upon the sky, so too our thoughts never affect the open, welcoming, accepting spaciousness of our consciousness, or awareness. Just as the sky must always accept each and every cloud, our consciousness will accept every thought, feeling, and sensation. Awareness doesn't judge them as good or bad, right or wrong. It can only accept them into the spacious awareness of our being.

If we are not the body, the thoughts, the feelings and sensations who or what are we?

Take a Moment: Contemplate Your Essence, Who You Really Are

All the qualities of Spirit are present in you, and are you right now.

You are not just a man or woman, a wife, husband, mother, father. You are not just the roles you play. You are not just your age, your history, your collection of experiences. You are an unlimited spiritual being, full of wisdom, peace, love, abundance, wholeness, and health. Your spirit has come to this planet, to your country, to your family, to this moment to experience what it is you are experiencing. Spirit has chosen to experience life in the myriad of circumstances, situations, and events of your life, right now.

▶ You are Health. You are experiencing unique relationships with health. What can you learn from this relationship with health that you are having right now? Can you remember that your spirit is free even when your body may be experiencing limitation?

▶ You are Love. You are experiencing a unique relationship with love. Where do you find love in your life? Where does it come from? Is it always given to you or do you give lots of love to others?

▸ You are Peace. You are experiencing a unique relationship with peace. When do you experience peace? Only when it's quiet? Only when someone reminds you? Do you carry peace with you wherever you go? Do you offer peace to others? Do you bring peace to other situations?

▸ You are Joy. You have a completely unique relationship with joy. Where is your joy? In your heart and soul? Are you joyful when you receive something from someone? Are you joyful simply because it is your true nature? Do you bring your joy with you into every situation?

▸ You are Abundance. You have a unique relationship with abundance. Do you recognize yourself as abundance? Do you see the abundance of Life in the stars, in the leaves of the trees, in the blades of grass in the fields? Do you experience yourself as enough? As more than enough? Do you know you are unlimited? Do you associate only with the limited body, the finite mind and resources?

You are an unlimited Spiritual Being, this is the truth of your Being. What does that feel like? Bring this feeling into your next activity, whatever it may be. And then do it again and again. You are Whole, perfect and complete, right now and always.

CHAPTER 10

Don't Believe Everything You Think

Remember when it was noted that the human mind thinks over 60,000 thoughts a day? Well, what if you believed all of those thoughts? It's a bit overwhelming, isn't it? This is why we feel swamped so often in our everyday lives.

So if you must believe everything you think, then think:

I am one with the Universe!

Everyone and everything I see are one with me!

The Universe supports my every move and desire!

Love is everywhere I look!

I am made in the nature and the likeness of God itself!

The entire universe conspires for my highest good and the good of all those around me!

I am happy and healthy!

I am surrounded by people who love and support me!

"The mind is a wonderful servant, but a terrible master."

−RAM DASS

Most of our thoughts come from the outside world of effects, from information processed through our senses; information we see and hear, like the so many noises from news, social media, so-called experts; information from well-meaning friends and neighbors, teachers, and politicians; information from advertisers, Big Pharma, insurance companies and health experts. Think about how inundated we were with the constant information regarding the COVID virus, and unfortunately much of the information contradicted itself!

Many of our thoughts come from our past, our memories and experiences. We take in a lot of information from the world out there, but often, the information is not true, or I should say, it is not the Truth. Some information may be factual, as in the recording of an event that transpired, but it may not represent the Truth of our Being.

"Thinking isn't a passive process unless you
do it passively. Thinking should always be an active
process where you think in a way that gets
you the results you want."

−RICHARD BANDLER

Often what we think are limiting thoughts and beliefs; when we believe those thoughts, we suffer. We are planting seeds of negativity, lack, and limitation. We believe people have hurt us; we believe they have wronged us. We think the world is crazy; we think there just isn't enough good to go around; we believe the reports that the economy is not favorable to us, that the government is corrupt, or that a pandemic has the ability to ruin our lives. Sometimes we think the weather sucks, just because it's raining. The weather is just being the weather. When we believe our thoughts about the weather, we may have a bad day because of our thoughts, not because of the weather!

Truth OR Consequences

The Truth is, we are always experiencing the consequences of our thoughts. It's more like truth *and* consequences! The mind is incredibly powerful. When the Buddha said the mind is everything, he meant what is held in mind often and with feeling will produce everything in your life. Our thoughts are things, and what we think, we become. In Proverbs we are told, "As a man thinks in his heart, so he is." And Jesus said, "It is done to you as you believe." Ernest Holmes made famous the saying, "Change your thinking, change your life."

What we believe, we are attracting repeatedly in our life, because what our beliefs are the seeds we are planting into the Law. They grow into the situations, events, and circumstances we are experiencing in our world of effects. We are continually experiencing the consequences of our thoughts. But we don't have to start monitoring our every thought, as if that would even be possible. When we take time each day to turn within and experience the Truth of our Being, that we are the spacious expansive sky or awareness, we align our thoughts with our intention; we experience more joy, more love, and more peace because we spend time *being* and *feeling* those qualities.

Einstein said, "The most important question one can ask is, is the Universe a friendly place?" Why? Why would this be the most important question? Because if we can answer with a resounding Yes!, if we believe the universe is a friendly place, then we will *experience* the universe as a friendly place. If we believe that sometimes it can be friendly, then we will experience our world as sometimes friendly and other times, not. If we answer no, the universe is harsh and cruel and unforgiving, then we are stuck in our own private hell. What do you believe about the universe? When we turn within, we always experience the Universe as Love, Joy, and Peace.

Pathways of Thought

A little science lesson: Neurologists now know that we create neural pathways in our bodies over the years. We create these pathways by choosing the same thoughts over and over again, which become beliefs, which become actions, which become the neural patterns of habits we experience in our daily life.

> "Whether you think you can, or think
> you can't—you're right."
>
> —HENRY FORD

We always have a choice, but many times it doesn't *seem* like we do, because we form habits which are quite strong and take almost no effort on our part to maintain. In other words, we don't THINK about what we are doing, because what we are doing has become a habit. It seems that we have no choice when we always, always have a choice.

Our habits can often require a lot of effort to break. And sometimes we aren't even sure why we believe what we believe. Someone told me that the quickest route to my work is the freeway. So I take the freeway. I always take the freeway. Out of the blue, I drive my sister to my workplace, and she looks up directions on Google Maps, and lets me know there is a much shorter route. What?! Why have I never looked? Because I tend to just believe whatever my thought is without doing my due diligence! In what areas of your life are you just blindly living? We create the box we live in with our habits, the out-picturing of our thoughts. The box is closed because our neural pathways are set, our actions are set. Our choices seem limited because we forgot that we don't have to believe everything we think! We believe we are smart, or pretty, or old, or ugly based on the information that comes at us from outside; newspapers, bosses, even tv commercials tell us we're not cool if we don't drive the right car! Michael Pirsner astutely asked, "How can we think outside the box when thinking *is* the box!" When we stop and *think*, we limit ourselves. When we stop and become Present, we uncover the Truth of our Being and we remember we are Unlimited!

When we turn within, we step outside the thinking mind, the box we've created, the habits we've created, and we realize that our thoughts are ours for the choosing. When we turn within and observe the thoughts, feelings, and sensations, we create the space to consciously choose something; otherwise, we continue to unconsciously follow along the neural pathways of ingrained patterns and habitual thinking. What will you choose today? Will you choose thoughts of health, abundance, friendship, loving relationships? Or will you unconsciously take the same path you've always taken?

"Your life is in your hands. No matter where you are now, no matter what has happened in your life, you can begin to consciously choose your thoughts, and you can change your life. There is no such thing as a hopeless situation. Every single circumstance of your life can change!"

—RHONDA BYRNE

How do we monitor, control, and look out for our thoughts? Once again, it's an inside job. We can go beyond any situation, into creative thought, into the spacious awareness of Consciousness. We can turn within right now and create the changes we wish to see in our lives. We can take 100% responsibility for what is happening in our life, our happiness, our joy, our health—no wiggle room! We let go of the past and using the past as an excuse or using fear of the future as an excuse. We step out of unconsciousness and we become mindful of the choices that are always available to us.

When we practice turning within and bringing the sense of Oneness and Wholeness into our everyday activities, we become aware of our thoughts and mindful of our actions.

We recognize how we create and participate in the day-to-day affairs of our lives. We become free to choose another thought, another seed to plant into the soil, the Law, and we sit back and rest in the knowingness of its fruition.

Our Past Choices Can Never Limit Us

Even though it seems as if those neural pathways are forged in some sort of cosmic iron, it is not true. We are never limited by what we have chosen previously. The sky is never limited by the clouds or storms that come and go. And newsflash: There are no limits on the Law. The All is not held hostage by our previous thoughts, or by any circumstances created by the human race. God Almighty is not a little mighty or some mighty, but Almighty. Do you think the Almighty is held hostage by the New York Stock Exchange? Do you think Infinite Spirit is limited by the things that happened to you as a child? Or the limited understandings of science? Spirit is available to us completely to lead us toward our highest good, even when we aren't sure what that looks like. It is never too late to change our mind, our thoughts, and plant a new seed to grow and create our paradise.

Take a Moment: Review Your Thought Inventory

What are the consequences you are experiencing now of your previous thinking? We can easily look at the situations, circumstances, and relationships in our life to discover the thought/seed that we have previously planted to create them.

▶ Close your eyes for a few minutes and take an inventory of your current experiences. Focus on one area of your life you would like to work on: your financial health, physical health, relationships, etc.

▶ Without judgment, write down your current state of affairs in this area. List just the facts, not the backstory. (i.e. I'm over-weight; I have high blood pressure; I have been feeling slow and sluggish lately.)

▶ Close your eyes and gently ask yourself, "What thoughts have contributed to these current results?" Perhaps the thoughts are from recent headlines or ancient voices. Where did these thoughts originate? When was the first time you heard them? Take your time and write them down in your journal.

▶ Look at them, each one. Ask yourself if those thoughts are serving you or limiting you.

▶ Decide, definitively, to let them go, replacing those thoughts with thoughts that support every aspect of your well-being.

▶ Close your eyes and ask your higher Self, "What are the thoughts that serve me best right now? Who am I now in this situation?"

▸ With eyes closed, see yourself planting these seeds, these powerful and positive thoughts, into the Law of Life that says, Yes!

▸ With your eyes still closed, imagine *how it feels* to live with these new thoughts revealing themselves as the new circumstances of your life. Feel what it's like to live in these changes. Feel the new consequences of your new thoughts. Feel the gratitude welling up within you.

Take some time each morning and evening to see yourself and feel yourself living these changes. Know that what you believe, you can achieve. Make it a habit to believe in yourself as renewed in this situation.

CHAPTER 11

The Good, the Bad, and the Enlightened

When we learn to pay attention to our thoughts and what we are thinking throughout the day, we come to realize that many of these thoughts are judgments, attachments, or resistance and reactions to things, ideas, or people. The ego always wants to label, categorize, and synthesize information. Its favorite activity is to judge things as good or bad, right or wrong, agreeable or disagreeable. It is constantly reacting to information without even hearing or understanding all the data. That's its job: to simplify the overload of information that comes in from the senses. Right now, is your mind agreeing or disagreeing?

Life Isn't Out to Get Us

Bad things aren't skulking around the corner waiting to pounce. Life is full of unique events and opportunities, but sometimes we seem to get caught up in what is really hard, challenging, or dreadful. What is it within us that is constantly judging things as "good" or "bad"? The ego.

Recently, I lived across from a preserve, a forest and swamp in Florida. It was beautiful with wild animals and all kinds of trees, flowers, and wildlife. There was a big lake in front and a swamp next to it. During a huge thunderstorm, I was looking out over the lake into the swamp and I saw a huge bolt of lightning hit a tree! It was mesmerizing! It was wild and powerful. It felt like my mind stopped, like one of those photographs of lightning frozen in time and space. I have that image emblazoned in my mind. What an awesome display of the power and beauty of nature. I wasn't afraid at all because it was a hundred feet away. I was in awe. However, it only took a few moments for my mind to take me back to my past during another huge thunderstorm when I lived in Southern California.

Intense thunderstorms in Southern California are rare, and this one brought lots of rain, lots of wind, and lots of lightning with nearby thunder. I heard a massive clap of thunder that made me jump and yell. I didn't see the lightning, but I definitely heard it and felt it; my hair was standing on end. Every television and computer and electrical outlet was fried and smoke was pouring out of them. I ran to the window, knowing the strike was somewhere right where I was, and saw my beautiful old sago palm in the back yard ablaze with smoke and fire. I called the fire department and prayed the flames wouldn't reach my house. I remember thinking, "Why did this happen to me? What did I do to deserve this? Why me?" The ego loves to wallow in these kinds of questions! Mine was wallowing away. My mind had already decided that it would take weeks to clean up the mess and a lot of money to replace the electronics and repair the damage.

What is the difference between lightning striking in a forest a perfectly safe distance away and it happening a few feet away, ruining my electronics and nearly burning down my home? None. Nothing. There is no difference. Lightning is being lightning. It can't be anything else. A storm is a storm. It wasn't out to get me or to impress me. However, our ego will judge one situation as bad and the other good because that's its job. The ego will take everything personally, because that's its main function. When we stop judging things as good or bad and we begin to see things for what they really are, we aren't burdened by a harsh life personally sabotaging us. We sense the awesomeness of all of Life, we understand that it is not personal, and we live free and enlightened.

Life-Threatening Situations

It's true: Life is just living itself, and sometimes there's an alligator in your swimming pool if you live in Florida! We can't ever stifle the ego, and if there is an alligator in your swimming pool, the ego will scream at you to run, jump, shoot, yell, hide, and probably ask one of those ridiculous ego questions, "Why in the hell did I move to Florida?" The ego is there to protect our body, our human container. It is never concerned with our spiritual Being. Fight-or-flight kicks in, and we can make life-or-death decisions instantly.

As I said, I have learned to be friends with my ego. Whenever it judges something, I thank it and ponder the validity of its judgement, from a more Whole perspective.

However, in the case of the alligator, running seemed like the very best option for all concerned. The truth is most often, we are not threatened by an alligator in the pool, or a bear in the backyard. We often do, however, feel threatened by our fears regarding the job market, the pandemic, the loss or potential loss of income, the fear of rejection from peers or loved ones. The ego treats these threats the same as the alligator or the bear: Judgment kicks in, fight-or-flight kicks in, and soon stress, resistance, and denial kick in. We believe the threat is as real and imminent as a snake in the living room and we fight or flee, all from the comfort of our chattering ego-mind.

Over time, this feeling of impending doom, the levels of stress, and the deterioration of our health multiply. We are sowing seeds of fear backed with emotion and anxiety into the great Law, the receptive soil, which says yes, be afraid. It says yes, these are insurmountable problems and gives you more seemingly insurmountable problems. It says yes, this is unhealthy and gives you worsening health. It can only say yes and give back to you what you are putting into it. When we become aware of our thoughts, we can choose to see them for what they are. We can choose to believe them or not.

The Good, the Bad

When we identify with our habitual thoughts (our perceptions, our beliefs), we are no longer identifying with divine Spirit, divine Purpose, or divine Self. This is why Eckhart Tolle describes the greatest obstacle to enlightenment as "identification with your mind, which causes thought to become compulsive."

When we label things as good or bad, when we are attached to things or resisting situations, we are enacting and enabling our old thought patterns to control us. If we label something as good, great, lucky, or blessed, we believe in its external power to make our lives better; that the thing, situation, person, or event has some power over us to make everything good or better. When we label or judge something as bad, we are enabling past conditioning to run things in the present moment.

JUDGMENTS

How many times have you sat in a meeting listening to someone speak while you're quietly commenting to yourself? Or you're watching a news program on TV and the voice in your head, your ego, is constantly commenting: "Yes, that's right. No way, I've never heard of that before. Who is this person anyway? She doesn't know what she's talking about. Why doesn't he get his story straight." On, and on, and on the ego-mind goes. You are so busy judging the person, the content, the clothes, the room, you aren't even present to *listen* to the content or be informed by it. You feel your blood pressure rise, a ball forms in the pit of your stomach, and you find yourself angry and upset or bored and blaming. We are rarely upset by the presenter; we are upset by our *thoughts about* the presenter.

When the ego is talking, we are not present and aware of what is actually transpiring on a deeper and more profound level. There may be ways for us to participate in the meeting on a spiritual, mental, or physical level, but we become incapable of sensing this because of our mind chatter. The chatter cuts us off from participating in the moment, from being available and creative, and we succumb to the numbing effects of ego-talk. Ego-talk is the committee of voices, the dialogues we have in our heads that seem to go on and on all by themselves. What is your mind telling you right now? Are you agreeing? Disagreeing? Or just being present?

ATTACHMENTS

We can find ourselves very attached to situations, people, or things, such as our youth, our job, our health, or our bank account. When we are attached to our looks, we will be disappointed when they change, as they most certainly will. I am not in the same body I was in 10 years ago, or 20 years ago, or even 5 years ago.

In Buddhism there is a saying: When you are attached to something, only one of two things will happen, it disappears, or you do. It means that nothing in the world of form is meant to last, not the sun, the moon, and certainly not the bank rate for the loan you just made. Our children grow up and we learn that they are not "ours". They have changed into independent adults right before our eyes, it seems. We may experience the opposite with our parents as they age. When we are attached to the level of health we are experiencing now, a sudden frightening diagnosis can devastate us. We go into shock as we lose the abilities we had in our body before, and we fight against what is.

While nothing prepares us for some of the sudden changes in our life, when we are practiced in the art of nonattachment, we flow with the events of our life with much greater ease and grace. When we are attached to one particular result of our activity, we suffer. If we work hard for a raise or promotion and we don't get that raise, we become upset and angry and can become miserable in a job that we once enjoyed. If we work hard because we value our work, we don't have to be attached to the result. We get the raise or promotion or we don't, but we have enjoyed our creative expression in our work.

Knowing and accepting that everything will change, we can enjoy the evolution of situations in our lives. If we don't get the promotion, we might eventually change jobs to match our level of energy and creativity, but we won't feel hurt, angry, or stressed out; we just move with the flow.

REACTIONS

Sometimes, in heated conversations, we may get a tight ball in the pit of our stomach, and before the person we are listening to is even finished speaking, we blurt out our rude reaction to what they are saying. Or we are yelling at the driver in the car next to us. Or grumbling through the entire morning because we stubbed our toe as we climbed out of bed. When we react to something, we are following along the neural pathways we created from all our previous choices. We aren't free, because we aren't choosing how to respond to the situation; instead we are engrossed in our *reaction,* which is conditioned. It is based on our history of reacting to similar events. There is no space in our heart or mind to allow the situation to unfold, giving us time to respond, rather than react. Reactions are habits. The enlightened take a moment to observe what is happening in the event, with the other person, in themselves, and then *respond.*

"Nothing in the world can bother you as much as your
own mind. In fact, others seem to be bothering you,
but it is not others, it is your own mind."

—SRI SRI RAVI SHANKAR

RESISTANCE

When we push against what is appearing in our life, we
actually create more of the same problems. What we resist
persists. Why? Because we are pushing against Life Itself. We
are pushing against what already is!

What we are resisting are the sprouts from the seeds we
have already planted and watched come into fruition. In
resisting, we are actually holding on to the thing we don't
want. Take, for example, the phrase *Fight Against Cancer*.
Cancer is still an epidemic in this country and fighting
against something often creates a fear and a possibility that
we can lose the fight. What about adopting the slogan Live
in Health! instead, with massive campaigns encouraging a
healthy lifestyle. When we take any negative campaigns in
our personal life and turn them into a positive ones, we stop
resisting and step into a place of power. We can look at other
examples such as the *War On Drugs*, or the war on anything
for that matter. When we turn that around to its opposite,
Live Free and Clear! we create a space for ourselves to take
creative control of our situations and not buy into common
limitations regarding illness, substance abuse, and even food
addictions. We can adopt our own personal life slogans and
forgo attention to the negative media.

"Always be for something, and against nothing."
—ERNEST HOLMES

This is a crucial point of personal power. Labeling something as so wrong that we want to use all our creative energy to fight against it most often makes the thing itself much more powerful in our lives. When we look at the examples from the current political and racial tensions, as well as the health crises presented by the COVID virus, we can see this enacted in 3D, graphically, and even violently on TV. We can see those who are fighting against what is and creating more and more violence and misunderstanding. At the same time, there are groups forming who are committed to honest communication, to understanding and resolving issues. This is a much more powerful and healthy place to be. It takes integrating spirit, mind, and body to live in this space in our personal lives.

We start with turning within, recognizing our true Nature, and living from that open, spacious awareness. We use our creative energy for something positive and powerful, and the Universe says, Yes!

When we plant the seeds of what we don't want, the Law can only say Yes! Here is what you don't want! Instead, we use our creative energy to promote positive changes for ourselves and our body of affairs, for our community, and for the planet. We state what we *do want*—love, joy, peace, prosperity—and allow Law to reveal *that* in our life. We get what we are, and when we are resisting and fighting, we get more of that. When we are in alignment with love and peace, we get more of that.

The Enlightened

The ego will judge; it will be fearful, it will resist change. That is its job description, but we will always have the choice to view our lives from our whole Self and see where we want to be spiritually, mentally, and physically. When we become still and quiet, we can feel and sense the signs and signals present in our physical, mental, and emotional bodies. Often, when we feel overwhelm, anxiety, and dis-ease, from our whole Self, we are inspired to take the steps to begin resolution and healing. When we feel overwhelmed, our ego voice is complaining, our body is exhausted, and we can't seem to get out from under the emotional feeling. With practice, we notice this and say, "Oh, ok, thank you, ego. I got this now. My whole and integrated Self will take care of this." Then we turn within, and we choose to release fear and accept Wholeness, health, and anything else we need to do to relieve the situation.

There is within us our highest Self, discerning what we need to do with the information the ego provides. We just don't want to leave it up to the ego. The ego will always react from a separated point of view. The Self will always respond from an enlightened point of view. We can always choose to live from our whole Self, our integrated Self.

Why does it seem difficult at times? Because when we are so identified with the smallness of our experience and we believe so much in our physical expression, we've lost touch with our Spirit. The Spiritual Self is whole, and the ego is a part, it can only see and identify a small part of our existence.

"That which is perfect" is our whole Self, and it is right where we are, now.

"We know in part, and we prophecy in part.
But when that which is perfect is come,
then that which is in part shall be done away."

—1 CORINTHIANS 9-10

Say Yes, Completely Accept the Present Moment

What does it feel like to let go of judgments, attachments, reactions, and resistance? It feels like a big, spacious sky which could never be disturbed by the clouds that come and go! When we learn to accept what is instead of labeling, pushing, denying, or resisting, we aren't caught up in the rantings of the ego and we go with the flow of life.

We are enlightened, always have been, always will be, and we remember to accept what is, right now in the present moment; then we turn within and allow ourselves to be guided from that place of peace and power to find solutions, healing, or answers to the situations in our life.

When we're not accepting what is, we're making it personal, as if life was out to get us. The spiritual practice of acceptance transforms the idea of feeling happy based on outside circumstances into actually being joyful or peaceful, regardless of circumstances. Joy and Peace are the qualities of Life which we each possess and which are never subject to external circumstances. We create so much personal suffering with our inability to accept what is.

When my son was very ill, I found myself saying often and enthusiastically, "I am exhausted." The thought quickly occurred to me, what if I said this a thousand more times? Would that make me feel better? More inspired, more rested? No, of course not. And really, was I exhausted, or was my body and my mind experiencing being overwhelmed and overtired?

The next time I felt my body feeling exhausted, I decided to lay down and really feel every inch of my weary body, my taut emotions, and my raging mind. I allowed myself to fully accept and surrender to the feeling, and honestly, it felt good. Breathing into this, I would then ask, "What does this exhaustion want to show me? What is here for me to look at? Am I working too hard on solving this problem? Do I think I, my small separate self, have to solve this? What can I do to take better care of me?"

When I allowed myself to feel the exhaustion and allotted the time for turning within, the enlightened answers would come. Gently, I would come to insights and understandings about the situation that would lift me and energize me and allow me to continue as a caregiver to my son.

I turned within, accepted the situation, and allowed myself the time and space to understand what the situation was telling me or teaching me. I couldn't change what was, but I could change my reaction to it. I could create a more vitalizing response in my body and mind, because I could choose my creative words, plant them in the soil, and replenish my spirit. I changed my thinking from "I am exhausted," to "I have the energy and resources I need to resolve this. I am strong and healthy. I am able to take care of myself and help my son. I am not alone." Those became my new seeds and I watched as they flourished in the garden of my life.

"Those who are free from attachment, fear, and anger—
and who have complete trust in me, become me."

—THE BHAGAVAD GITA

In enlightenment, we accept what is as if we had chosen it. Why? Because it *already is*. It already exists in our life. And what if we had chosen it? What if you had chosen illness to heal yourself or others, or to know that you are more than your body, more than your dis-ease? What if you had chosen poverty to learn prosperity? What if you had chosen to break up with your lover, spouse, or partner to learn that your true source of Love could never leave you? What if you had chosen limitation, addiction, or abuse to learn that you are more than the situations, events, and circumstances in your life? What are the lessons, as spiritual beings, that we are to learn from our most formidable teachers in this world? When we accept what is, we engage our peaceful and harmonious mind, revitalize our body, and out of that we learn, we grow, we transcend suffering and become stronger, more powerful, more joyful human Beings.

The enlightened do not escape human feelings and emotions. The difference is in the way they deal with what is before them. Everything any one of us experiences is a gift. Every. Single. Thing. Sadness, exhaustion, depression, anger, frustration, as well as happiness, pride, a sense of accomplishment, joy, etc. These are all pointers to what we are participating in and what we need to focus on to help us grow and evolve. When we accept what is, we allow ourselves to expand and move through it. When we resist what is, we quickly become very stuck and we temporarily lose the ability to be informed by what is to help us regain balance and harmony.

"In the depths of winter, I finally realized that there was in me an invincible summer."

—ALBERT CAMUS

There is the Unlimited Consciousness within us that remains Whole, perfect and unaffected by the many circumstances in our life. It is our Self, our Source, our very Essence. When we accept and turn within, we give ourselves the time and space to connect with this Wholeness, and we bring this "invincible summer" into every aspect of our life. When we practice accepting the moments as they come, we are practicing Wholeness. And Spirit always moves us into a greater and greater expression of this unity.

"When we let go and let God, we are creating a
spiritual practice so powerful that the core beliefs
that have held us captive and small are dismantled,
resistance to our good melts away, fear of the
unknown is shattered, a sense of oneness with God
and all life is embodied, and a whole new world
of infinite possibilities opens up for us."

—DIANE HARMONY

Acceptance is Powerful—Not Passive

Acceptance is an inner spiritual practice. It is powerful, not passive. There are some interesting misconceptions about acceptance that are important to go over.

Acceptance is not:

resignation,

apathy (not caring or being concerned),

passively putting up with situations in life which are uncomfortable,

doing nothing,

positive thinking (although positive thinking is a type of training for accepting what is).

Acceptance is a choice for spiritual, mental, and physical well-being. Eckhart Tolle calls it "yielding to Life rather than opposing It." As we live enlightened, we let go of the judgments, attachments, resistance, and reactions and instead see that there is something bigger that contains all of what we label. It takes seeing from a fresh perspective, an enlightened perspective, to live in harmony with all of life that surrounds us.

The enlightened know to resist the ego's tendency for judgments, attachments, resistance, and reactions. We stay out of the JARR and instead, we listen from the alert awareness of enlightenment, and we discern intuitively whether something is right for our life. We can choose to create situations, relationships, and self-expression without being attached to them. We can stop reacting to people and events and instead, take the time to respond from an enlightened perspective.

In the midst of extreme political discord, great racial tension, heightened fear for our health and well-being, such as during the pandemic, we are called to turn within and pull forth from within our peace, our discernment, our compassion and understanding. It is easy in early spiritual development to think we must turn away from the world and to sit in our "closet" and meditate all day. But that is not living enlightened. It is hiding our light. When we integrate spirit, mind, and body, we are able to bring the peace that passes all understanding into the situations and events of our everyday life. We become the conduit for peace and acceptance in the situations we find ourselves. We become a place of refuge in the storm of a messy life. We bring a sense of order to the chaos.

There is an interesting phenomenon that happens when we become accomplished in the art of letting go of judgments, attachments, reactions, and resisting. We don't act according to the way many people believe we should act!

When we give up judgments, we may seem to others ignorant of the importance of the situation. When we give up attachments, we may seem uncaring or indifferent. When we give up reactions, we may seem uninterested or less passionate. When we give up resisting, we may seem apathetic.

The Truth is, when we give up these things, we are in a deep state of harmony with Life. We are living from our Whole Self rather than the ego or emotional self. We experience Peace, the peace that passes human understanding, because it is our Spiritual nature.

It is important to stay aligned with awareness so that we are not swayed by how we seem to others and instead we rest in a complete Oneness with everything life wants to bring. And remember not to judge others for how they may judge us!

Take a Moment: Imagine Accepting Life on Life's Terms

Stay out of the JARR and accept what is, knowing that you have within yourself the creative power to respond rather than react to life. You can choose to not be a soccer ball, being kicked around by all the events in life; instead you choose to stay centered in yourself, and affect the outer world with your inner peace, love, and genuine acceptance.

Take a few deep cleansing breaths and gently ask yourself:

▸ What am I resisting in my life right now? What am I judging as bad, as wrong, as fearful?

▸ Now, imagine yourself in this situation, fully involved. In your mind, see who is around and really sense the ego thoughts as they would arise in this particular situation. Just notice how this event usually unfolds.

▶ Now, decide to accept it fully. Imagine yourself in this same situation and accepting it. See yourself being in the situation without judgment, without attachment to it being gone or different, without reactions, without resisting. Imagine saying, "Ok, I surrender, I accept."

▶ Ask yourself, "What would you have me do with this now?"

▶ Say out loud, "I accept this as my experience right now and everything it brings to my life. Even while I am experiencing this, I allow this to empower me and those around me." It might look like this: "I accept that I am experiencing (a flu, a virus, a cancer) in my body right now and all the situations it brings to my life. I allow my true nature of health to empower me in this, and my inner strength and guidance empowers all those around me."

▶ Take some time to envision the good that this event has brought with it. For example, you might say, "I feel supported by friends and family, even while my body is sick. I am sensing the healing in my mind and body. I am grateful for my life, my family, and the many blessings that are present in my life right now."

Remember that acceptance is an inner spiritual practice; it is powerful, not passive. It allows for powerful resolutions to any and all of life's challenges.

Write down in your journal any insights or revelations from this meditation. Go through this practice once or as many times as you need to realize a complete healing.

CHAPTER 12

What's Your Story?

What's your story? Inquiring minds want to know!

The True story is: We are human animals, and we are spiritual Beings. We are human Beings! We are unlimited Spiritual Beings made in the image and likeness of God Itself, full of wisdom, peace, love, abundance, Wholeness, and health. We also acknowledge that we are a unique member of humanity, appearing at this point in time, in this particular body, with our unique situations, events, and circumstances.

Our Unlimited Spiritual Potential has shown up in this seemingly confined, limited small space we call a body. We are born and have a name; we had events happen to us, either good or bad depending on our point of view or the points of view of others around us. We have known beauty and joy and experienced pain and suffering in combinations that make us unique and unlike anyone else on the planet.

Perspective is Everything

When I was turning 50, I was very happy having circled around the sun for 50 years, surrounded by friends and family. My brother who I am close to had survived cancer; my son was healthy and creative, and I was loving life. I was experiencing relative health and prosperity, and all in all I was excited to celebrate half a century on the planet! I planned a small party, a girls night out, and several lunch dates. Life was good. I soon found out that an acquaintance of mine was turning 50. She was very agitated and unhappy. She complained that her body couldn't do the things that it used to, that she didn't look like she used to, that her husband didn't treat her like he used to, that her kids were grown and ignoring her; there were a lot of judgments and attachments! She was miserable and wasn't going to celebrate one thing. And she really wanted me to commiserate with her... How interesting! We had similar life events, but not similar reactions, not at all.

"Some suffer, some are happy, some unhappy, according to the way they contact life. No one judges us but ourselves. No one gives to us but ourselves and no one robs us but ourselves."

—ERNEST HOLMES

We have a history of stories we tell ourselves and others. "Oh, you think that's bad, you should hear what happened to me." Or, "You think your relationship was bad, let me tell you about mine." We often let our stories define us.

To know someone well is to know their stories, the experiences that have shaped them, the trials and turning points that have tested them. When we want someone to know us, we tell our stories. I am a father, husband, salesman, breadwinner; I am sick, strong, weak, well. I am 50. I am old. I am beautiful. I am a mother. I am successful, unlucky, brave, boring, athletic, competitive, sentimental, sensitive. We have so many stories to back up who we are, and have you noticed we will repeat these stories over and over? The more we identify with our story, the more stories we create to keep and hold on to our ego identity.

What happens when we live enlightened, live fully as a Spiritual Being having a human experience, instead of living our lives as a human being searching for some spiritual meaning?

When your sense of who you are is not your job, your looks, your name, or your accomplishments or failures–when your sense of who you are is All There Is–you live enlightened.

"If you want to fly in the sky, you need to leave the earth. If you want to move forward, you need to let go the past that drags you down."

–AMIT RAY

When we come to know ourselves as not just our stories, we come into a fuller understanding that the physical world is not all there is. We are not our history, our past, and our circumstances. We are not even this body. This body isn't the same as it was yesterday or a few years ago. It is easy to see that I am not who I was at 7, or 27, or 47. Scientists estimate there are around 37 trillion cells in the body. Each type of cell has its own life span. Red blood cells live for about four months, while white blood cells live more than a year on average. Skin cells live about two or three weeks. Our bodies have regenerated and changed hundreds of times!

"The Self, which is God, dwells in every being, but only those with wisdom and perception—having the ability to hold the mind steady—will recognize this. When the senses obey the mind, God will be revealed."

—THE KATHA UPANISHAD

There is a process that happens in our search for the Spiritual Truth. It begins when we reveal and tell a new story, the True story. We uncover the story about our True Nature and we allow experiences into our lives that support the True story. We deny into our lives things that would have supported the old, limited story. Can you imagine your spiritual Being free and whole in complete joy right now? What will it take to let go of the story? When we decide to, we can simply let it go, like an old blanket that has served its purpose, and focus on the Truth. What will it take to let go of the story that limits you?

The story of Paul in the gospel is one of the most compelling descriptions of changing one's story. Paul's name was originally Saul. He was a Jewish soldier zealously persecuting early followers of Jesus, defending traditional Judaism. As written in Acts 9, Saul was on the road to Damascus when a light and a voice struck him down. He heard the voice of Jesus ask him, "Saul, why do you persecute me?" Saul was blinded and deeply confused. In Damascus, he stayed in a room for 3 days in what we can imagine was ardent self inquiry. When he emerged, he had completely changed his thoughts, his direction in life, and his story. Saul changed his name to Paul and began speaking the word of the Christ Consciousness almost immediately. Paul had never met Jesus, but he was so transformed by his inner experience of light and truth, that he changed the course of history. Paul did not spend time in agony over his mistakes. He didn't waste one moment dwelling in his old story, but instead created a new one with Love at the center of it. Imagine if he had spent time in regret, in apologizing, in agonizing over his previous serious faults. He shed his old story, like a snake sheds its skin, and he was renewed. He became the most ardent supporter of Jesus and helped to create Christianity.

I had a client who, when I first met him at one of my workshops, told me he moved here for better schools for his special-needs daughter. I asked him how that was working out. "Not well," he said. "I don't know many people, and it's hard to get around this city. It's so big. We haven't met any other families who are in a similar situation, and we really miss the farm and the outdoors." He was pretty despondent. I tentatively asked, "Other than the possibility of a better school, have you found anything else you like about Jacksonville?" His face lit up, "Yes, there is so much water! The ocean, the river, the lakes, the tributaries. My daughter loves going to the ocean, playing in the waves and the sand,

and we saw a manatee in the river just yesterday!" He was beaming with excitement at the memory.

After the workshop on changing your story, he came up to me and asked if I meant it literally. "Do I literally change my story?" I answered, "Well, yes! In your case, instead of leading your introduction with what is wrong, with what is disappointing, or what the problems are, perhaps you could begin your story with how you and your daughter love the ocean and being surrounded by water and the great programs in the school system." He looked doubtful but said he would give it a try. I saw him two weeks later, and he seemed completely changed! He told me he had met families with similar needs who had embraced him and his daughter in support. He said that all he did was change his story! He introduced himself with his love for the ocean and the possibility of better school conditions for his daughter and others embraced and welcomed him. His whole countenance changed. He was enthusiastic about new possibilities.

Sometimes we are shy about telling our story, so we just agree with the stories of those around us. Do you find yourself agreeing with others that life is hard, or this is the worst year ever, or the economy will never recover? Do you find yourself nodding in agreement that these people are right, and those people are wrong, even when you may not believe that story? The ego wants to fit in and doesn't want to be challenged. And that's ok, except when we are creating pain and suffering for ourselves and others. Every time we nod our head in agreement with a story of lack and limitation, we are sowing those seeds, and we will reap what we sow. We don't have to stand up to our boss, or our parent, or the political extremists if we aren't called to, but we don't have to agree with them either. With an open and compassionate heart, we find our strength in the Truth, rather than the story.

"Let go of your story so the Universe
can write a new one for you."
—MARIANNE WILLIAMSON

What we believe is our particular perception; our perception becomes our reality, but it is never the Truth. What is the Truth? When the light within me sees, honors, loves, and appreciates the light with in you, because I know we are the rays of the one and only sun, we experience the Truth.

Who would you be without your story? If you are not your ego-mind, your history, or your body, who are you? You are an unlimited Spiritual Being, full of wisdom, peace, love, abundance, Wholeness, and health!

Yes, literally change your story to include your magnificence!

Imagine you have amnesia and you couldn't remember your story. You would wake up, go outside, and start exploring. Like a child, you would explore your environment and find things you love and things that don't really excite you. Eventually you would be exposed to people on bikes, people walking or running in the neighborhood or on the mountain trails or beaches, and you might think, "That looks like fun," or, "I would never do that!" You would be exposed to tennis and golf, race-car driving and horseback riding, airplanes and astronauts. Some things would excite you or interest you and some wouldn't. But it would all be based on who you are right now, in this moment, and not what you have tried before and failed at or even what you have been successful in and stuck with, even though deep down you may not like it that much. Looking at things as if we had never seen them, never experienced them, never even heard about them, gives us a new perspective. Turning within and allowing our creative sense to dictate what we gravitate toward and away from is always in alignment with our highest good of who we are now.

Let go of the story. Let go of the results from your past. Let go of your fears of failing or succeeding. When we're aligned with our highest good, we move forward into aligned choices and aligned action. And we will always experience joy from that alignment.

Take a Moment: Imagine Changing Your Story

What is the story you tell the most? And what is the story you would really like to share?

▶ Think about how you introduce yourself to others. What story do you tell? Does it focus on what you do? Or who you are? Does it reflect the whole of you or just some limited aspect of your life? Does it reflect who you know yourself to be in your heart?

▶ Where you can, change the details of the story you've been telling. Remember, you are not denying what is; you are accepting but changing the focus of the story to something powerful and positive. Focus on including a positive event, a recent insight, a healing.

Take some time to look within and find other stories you tell about yourself. Do you often go over a childhood incident? The unfair incident that happened at work 5 years ago? Are there other stories you tell often? Are there stories you agree with?

Rewrite and retell your story to focus on something powerful and positive. Try it out on family, friends, and at work.

CHAPTER 13

Who Are You Really?

I f you are not your story, then who are you?

If we are not our story, our descriptions, our body, or our collection of memories, then who are we? Who are you? Who is this self?

> "Happiness is our true nature, and we cannot be truly happy until we know who we really are."
>
> —SRI RAMANA MAHARSHI

Our stories are what has happened to us. The story IS NOT WHO WE ARE. The events, circumstances, and relationships in our life don't define who we are; they are things we experienced. We have thoughts about them. We may remember them accurately or inaccurately, but they are events experienced by us. The Truth is that we, our innermost Beings, have never been hurt, harmed, or endangered.

Who is the one who remembers? Who is the one who is thinking the story? Who is the one who is aware of the thinking? We would call this simply Presence, or Awareness, or Self. The reason I capitalize these words is because they are not limited or confined to our human existence, or our ego-self. This is our True Nature, or our Consciousness. When we stop trying to become what we think we are and simply uncover who we were born to be, we are authentic and enlightened.

"Seek out that particular mental attribute which makes you feel most deeply and vitally alive, along with which comes the inner voice which says, 'This is the real me,' and when you have found that attitude, follow it."

—WILLIAM JAMES

What happens when we live as a Spiritual Being having a human experience rather than living our lives as a human being searching for some fleeting spiritual meaning? The greatest joy is in being an authentic whole Self, a human Being! Being completely and unabashedly me. Being wholly and holy you. We eliminate the voices in our head that tell us what we should be doing, what we should want, what we are and are not capable of, and instead, turn within and hear the voice of who we really are: the child of the Most High. With enlightenment comes authenticity and the ultimate expression of our uniqueness.

"Not only is every individual an incarnation of God, and therefore a manifestation of Christ, but since each individual is unique, every person has access to God in a personal sense. The Spirit is most certainly personal to each one of us individually and uniquely personal. We could not ask for a more complete union than this for the union is absolute, immediate, and dynamic."

—ERNEST HOLMES

Sometimes we only have a moment when the voices in our head are silent. In that moment, the Universe speaks and tells us everything we need to know! I am who thou art, and thou art who I am.

Who Am I?

One day I was sitting, meditating, my legs neatly crossed in a half lotus position, breathing deeply, slowly, in and out, my arms extended over my knees and my hands in a relaxed mudra, I breathed in and out, again and again. Anyone watching might have said I was deep in meditation, breathing in, breathing out, sahaj samadhi, but inside my head, there was a different scenario. My mind was going a mile a minute, something like this: "How can I have time to meditate with all the things I forgot to do, need to do, should do, should have already done? Is that my stomach grumbling. I'm hungry. What's in the fridge? Nothing, ughh. I forgot to go to the store. Great, now I have to remember to add going to the grocery store to my list. Wait, where's my list? Uuuggghhh. Great, now I have to add find my list to a new list." And then I (another "I") said, "STOP. Please stop. For the love of God, be quiet!" Then there was silence, deep silence. I took another deep breath in, let it go, and another, ahhh, and another. The mind raced on: "What time is it? Has it been an hour? Feels like an hour. Ugghhh, I should've eaten before I meditated. C'mon you can't eat before you meditate, you'd be full. You can if it's salad or carrots." Then the voice said rather loudly, "OH MY GOD— COULD YOU PLEASE BE QUIET? ALL OF YOU, JUST BE QUIET." Whew, and there was silence again, deep, deep silence and stillness.

It was in the deep stillness that it came to me, not as a voice or a thought but an experience: I am my Source revealed—I am my Source revealed. More silence. I felt: All There Is is revealed as me, here, now…. Always and forever, the Source of All There Is is revealed in me now. All that has ever been and all that will ever be is revealed in me, as me, now.

All the Love, Joy, Peace, Happiness, Abundance, and Prosperity there is and ever was is revealed in me now. Every discovery in science, every great piece of art and architecture, every technological discovery, every philosophical insight and physical adventure is within me, is me, now. Infinite possibility is revealed in me now. All that I know of God, and everything I don't, is revealed in me, is me, now.

I am my Source revealed.

You are the Source Revealed

Creation decided to put itself in a body and have a seemingly confined experience in this time-space continuum and showed up as me, as Elizabeth, and as you, exactly who you are, where you are, and how you are, unlimited in possibility and only confined by perceptions that seem real. There is in fact only One Source, and there is only One Event that is always taking place: Life creating Itself as All There Is.

When we follow our enlightenment, turn within, and commune with Spirit, we reclaim our true identity and we integrate spirit, mind, and body. Our divine identity is revealed in us and inspiring ideas flow through us and we revel in it all. We are the only way the All There Is expresses Itself. Spirit will never again express through you, as you, like this right now. This is it!

Letting go of all of our limiting identities and beliefs about ourselves lightens us up so we may "be" in the manner that Spirit, as us, wishes to express. We are the only expression of God that exists like us! We are unique and unbelievably extraordinary! The All There Is will never happen again like you or like me, so we must find our fullest expression of who we are right now.

We can define passion as a strong feeling of enthusiasm or excitement for something or about doing something. As we step into enlightenment, our genuine passions and the ways to support them are revealed to us clearly. We remember that our true identity is not what we do, who we are with, what we look like, where we live, our history, or any other factor of our humanity. Who we are is a divine emanation of Spirit and nothing less. By living enlightened, the answers to career, income, relationships, health, all the most important aspects of our human experience become clearer.

Our purpose is that which brings us joy and creates harmony while we are doing it. When we are actively fulfilling our divine purpose, we give joy back into our relationships, our community, and our world. Our Divine Identity comes in whispers and in nuance. It comes to us as ideas at work and through the forging of new relationships. It comes to us in meditations and in the lyrics of a song on the radio. When we listen closely and take the time to be still, in the stillness we will hear the deafening truth of who we are.

"We are here to awaken from the illusion of our separateness."

−THICH NHAT HANH

What no longer serves you, no longer allows you to express your joy? We always get what we say yes to, and the opposite is also true. Say no to what is no longer serving your highest good and you will be saying yes to your authentic Self. Eliminate the voices in your head that tell you what you should be doing, what you should want, who you should be. Instead, turn within and hear the Voice of who you really are.

Anita Moorjani, who wrote *Dying to Be Me*, believed the whole reason for her journey into death was to deliver the message for us to become fully our authentic Self. Let's face it, in the human realm, we are always going to have our roles to play with differing ideas and levels which we adapt to the roles. We are daughter and mother and executive, father, brother, teacher. Ultimately we are moving toward expressing more of our God-Self, our authentic Self in each and every situation, without letting the external situations dictate who we are. We are not creating ourselves anew; we are revealing more of the Truth that has always existed as us. We aren't creating a new mask; we are letting go of the many different masks and revealing our true identity.

"Our endeavor, then, is not so much to find God, as it is to realize God's Presence and to understand that this Presence is always with us. Nothing can be nearer to you than that which is the very essence of your being. Your outward search culminates in the greatest of all possible discoveries—finding God at the center of your own being."

—ERNEST HOLMES

Take a Moment:
Explore Who You Really Are

When we turn within and ask, "Who am I?", the point isn't to find an answer, because any answer is just a concept. Eventually, or suddenly, you will experience who you are as a Spiritual Being, free, without a story, without ideas and concepts.

▶ Breathe deeply and gently ask yourself, "Who am I?" As an answer comes, just allow it to fall away or dissolve. Gently ask again. Who am I really?

▸ Write down any answer that comes, even if they are old concepts of yourself. Name, age, occupation, history, description; keep writing until there is a space in the thoughts.

▸ Then take a few deep breaths and just be still in that space.

▸ Feel the Presence, the Essence of who you are, without words and concepts.

Take Another Moment: Explore How Spirit Reveals Itself Through You

When we know that we are our Source revealed, we realize Spirit reveals Itself through our every activity and is our very essence. How does Spirit reveal uniquely as you?

Take a few deep centering breaths.

▸ Ask yourself: How does Creative Source want to reveal through me, now?

▸ Does Spirit reveal Itself through your laughter, your creativity?

▸ Does Spirit reveal Itself through your being organized, your thoughtfulness, your wisdom?

▸ Does Spirit reveal Itself through your nurturing, your dedication, your compassion?

▶ Is there something new wishing to express through you?

▶ Is there something to let go of, something that is no longer serving you?

▶ Allow yourself to linger in the silences and to rest on any images or thoughts that arise.

Write down any images, ideas, revelations, or insights in your journal.

CHAPTER 14

Be the Archeologist— Uncover Hidden Beliefs, Trash, and Treasure

D oes it ever feel like once you have decided to change, to grow, to evolve, you end up staying the same? You have honestly made the decision to be more, to really rise up out of your current circumstances, to live enlightened. And yet, as you meditate, pray, journal, or take a class, workshop, or retreat to move toward this wonderful new goal (what you hoped would help), you are still feeling stuck.

Spirit is always calling us to be a greater expression, but what do we do when we say yes to growth and it feels like the Universe is saying NO back? In this case, there may be some deep, underlying issues standing in our way that we are consciously unaware of. We can be praying and affirming consciously while our subconscious is clinging to hurts or resentments, negative or limited ideas based on our past experiences. When we are doing the work, committing to daily practices, and consciously shifting our habits and patterns but not seeing the movement toward growth and expansion we believe could be happening, we can turn within and shine some conscious light into our deep interior life.

"Our lives are products of our mind. What we are today is a result of what we thought yesterday. What we think today influences what happens to us tomorrow."

—THE DHAMMAPADA

I sometimes envision my life as a path, and occasionally I am called to go back and visit a rock or a boulder that was in my path many years ago to see if I am still unconsciously clinging to limiting beliefs surrounding it, or even carrying the giant boulder up the hill with me.

Periodically we may need help delving into a past painful experience. Many times we think to ourselves, "I've already dealt with that, I've already learned my lessons, forgiven myself and others;" *that is the ego talking.* Like our spiritual evolution, our understanding of our pain is evolving too. We may have another layer of learning, another layer of healing, of forgiveness to go through so we can continue to grow and evolve.

When we are consciously prayerful and excited and working toward our spiritual revolution, but not moving forward, our subconscious beliefs and perceptions of past events could be causing us to experience a house divided.

If we are blocked, we may have some incongruent thoughts happening; consciously we are saying yes to an expression of more love, but our relationship is falling apart; we say yes to more prosperity, but the credit card companies are hounding us and we fear we may have to declare bankruptcy; we say yes to more creativity at our job and we are fired, unceremoniously, and without severance! How is this our growth and evolution? Ram Dass said, "If you want to see how enlightened you are, spend a week with your family." He was alluding to the fact that even the most serene and enlightened being may turn into an insecure middle child when surrounded by a deeply rooted family dynamic once again.

"A man sees in the world what he carries in his heart."

—JOHANN WOLFGANG VON GOETHE

As we allow ourselves to revisit and explore past events, we uncover significant blocks to our attempts to reveal our true essence. Once we discover these blocks, we can shine the light of love, forgiveness, compassion, and Truth on them, freeing up our energy to continue to transform in Spirit. In any case, we can be very sure some negative or limiting thoughts are subconsciously planted in the creation process and they may be diametrically opposed to what we wish to experience in our life right now.

When I know and accept that it is done to me as I believe, it's a good time to ask, what do I believe? With the pandemic, I've been focused on health, staying healthy, and releasing any fear of getting sick. With all the confusing news and information, I had this realization—not a new one, just a very relevant one—that the study of medicine is oddly just that. It is the study of the pills to take and procedures to do to block the symptoms and situations in our body that are causing us disease, discomfort, or pain.

But what if it were the study of health? What if our society spent years and decades studying what health is, where it comes from, how to achieve it? Perfect health is an idea in the mind of Creation, of Source. We are told that we are made in the image and likeness of God itself, so there must be that perfect idea of man and woman in the Mind of Spirit. And not just any man or any woman, but each of us; we are the individualized expression of the One. There is a perfect idea of each of us, our perfect expression, and therefore our perfect health. But when something appears in our body to cause disease or pain, can we *believe* that we are healthy despite appearances to the contrary? How do we accept what is, the experience of being unhealthy, and know at the same time that *there is perfect health?*

As we've learned thus far, we don't deny what is happening in our body or in our life, but we don't have to own it as part of us either. We can actually own the idea of our perfect health; it is ours. One Mind created us with the idea of perfect health. The most powerful belief is the one that recognizes this. It is one thing to use our imagination to see or sense ourselves as healthy; that is a good start. But we are told in mystic teachings that we must believe that we are healthy *now*. It is done unto us as we believe. And we have the power to believe in things that we cannot see, imagination coupled with faith. When we experience any kind of disease or discomfort, we can know the Truth for ourselves; there is the perfect idea in the mind of God, the perfect idea of health for our lungs, our eyes, in any part of the body that is experiencing disorder. We can believe and have faith in healing.

"Faith is being sure of what we hope for,
and certain of what we do not see."

—HEBREWS 11:1

Exploring Past Limiting Beliefs

When I was very young, I was told to put on sunscreen so I wouldn't get cancer. I grew up in Florida and I was a competitive swimmer, and a lifeguard. How many times did I put on sunscreen so I wouldn't get cancer? Countless times. Eventually, I just put on sunscreen and the thought behind it became buried in my subconscious. Well, I experienced cancer, melanoma, on my arm.

When I was diagnosed, I began to question. What if I had learned to put on sunscreen so that I could enjoy healthy skin the rest of my life? I never *consciously* thought about it, but eventually I realized that every time I was putting on sunscreen, there was an unconscious thought about cancer! If I had learned earlier the practice of mindfulness, becoming aware of my actions, and the thoughts behind them, perhaps I wouldn't have experienced melanoma.

I was told to brush my teeth so I wouldn't get cavities,

so my teeth wouldn't fall out. That was my parents' way of giving us incentive to brush our teeth. Yikes! What if they taught us to brush our teeth so we could enjoy healthy teeth for the rest of our lives? We are told to exercise so we don't atrophy, get stiff, age, or to lose weight.

What if experts told us to exercise so we could enjoy strong, powerful, flexible bodies for the rest of our lives? Wouldn't we have a different unconscious belief behind these actions?

I have automatically done many things so that I don't experience illness or disease, but the *thought of illness and disease* was always right there, subconsciously, in those activities.

Now is the time to uncover and release any negative hidden and subconscious beliefs behind our actions. It is right now that we can remind ourselves that we are born in the image and likeness of perfect Health, so that our thoughts stay on health. How much more powerful would that be?

We could spend years with hidden negative images of cavities, of cancer or ruined skin, of getting old, of lack and limitation, or we can look into our activities, become aware of our habits, uncover hidden beliefs, and replace them with powerful, positive ones.

Today, right now, we can use a new idea, words backed with passionate emotion, to create powerful images of health and well-being, replacing any images of sickness and limitation. We can believe in our health, our prosperity, our self worth, and anything else we desire. We can remember to not identify with any illness or discomfort. We can remember the Truth of our Being, that health and wellness and vitality at any age is our birthright. What happens to us is not who we are; it is an experience we have.

When I did experience cancer, because of these teachings, I knew it was not the Truth of who I am. I could say that I experienced cancer; it was something that happened to me, but it isn't the Truth of me. I acknowledged that I didn't have cancer; it wasn't mine and I don't own it, but it was something I was experiencing in my body. We never deny what we are experiencing, but we don't have to own the experiences as our identity either. Just like the things that happened to me when I was 7 or 17 are not who I am now. They are things I experienced.

We can use this process of uncovering any hidden beliefs that may play out subconsciously in any area of our lives. Perhaps we spend money beyond our means or we are painfully thrifty and frugal. We may attract or repel certain types of relationships or jobs and repeat situations over and over again.

We have to be the archeologist and uncover hidden beliefs surrounding the habits and recurring situations in our life. These are the beliefs we once ingested, perhaps a very long time ago, like with the sunscreen and cancer, and now only the habit remains. They are false beliefs we have adopted and turned into our own subconscious beliefs which may be working against us. I can hear the voices of my past saying, "I have to save for a rainy day. When will the other shoe drop. There aren't enough hours in the day. You'll get sick if you don't put on a sweater."

The negative thought survives beneath the level of our awareness. When we become mindful of our thoughts, our feelings, and our habits, we can determine what the subconscious and underlying beliefs behind them are and we can let them go or change them.

When we are planting the seeds of new growth, if we have good seeds, seeds from a healthy crop (i.e. an aligned intention), and we plant the seed, we water, and there is enough sun, enough time, and still no results, we need to look under the topsoil. Perhaps the ground below is too rocky with events that we need to sort through and heal. Perhaps the ground underneath is too soggy with negative thought, drowning out the new growth. Or perhaps we've riddled the ground with the weeds of our past beliefs in limitation or lack. When something is not coming to fruition which we have consciously chosen, we need to look at the underlying thoughts that are certainly blocking our good. It isn't always easy to identify within our mind where the problem lies, but it will be made clear when we remember; it's an inside job, and we turn within to Spirit.

"We are responsible for what we are,
and whatever we wish ourselves to be,
we have the power to make ourselves."

—SWAMI VIVEKANANDA

Big Girls Don't Cry

Sometimes on our journey of growth and evolution we have traumatic experiences. Our culture often demands that we just get over it: Big boys don't cry. Just suck it up. Don't cry over spilt milk, etc. We may get some ill-founded advice to ignore our pain, or "just let it go" as we hear so often in spiritual circles. But many times, what we think we've let go of is stuffed deep into our subconscious. We bury some part of ourselves, and in truth, we are not really Whole without that part. We now know with the study of psychology that shoving pain, fear, blame, guilt, and shame under the proverbial rug is very detrimental to our mental health. It is detrimental to our spiritual evolution as well.

"Choosing the path of wisdom, become aware
of those things which lead you forward,
and those which hold you back."

—BUDDHA

When the seeds of our earnest thoughts are not returning to us multiplied and abundant, our frustration pushes us to dig deep into our memories for things we thought we had already released, buried, or swept under the rug. We talk to the little girl or boy who was devastated by a childhood event; we remember an embarrassing teenage moment; we recall the pain of an illness or the devastation of loss; we remember the harm we inflicted on others along the way. Self-forgiveness is only part of the solution.

Besides forgiving ourselves, we must forgive others and allow ourselves to love again and nurture those aspects of ourselves as we would a dear, close friend we haven't seen for a long time. As we reconnect with all the aspects of ourselves, we can feel Whole again. This will give us new insights and a new understanding of how the past and our limiting perceptions and beliefs have been holding us back. From that moment, we'll be able to move forward with power and positivity once again.

"Nothing ever goes away until it has taught us what we need to know."

—PEMA CHÖDRÖN

Take a Moment:
Uncover Hidden Beliefs

When we ask our ego why we don't have something we want, or why we aren't experiencing something we've set our sights on, it will often give us very helpful clues as to the old patterns of beliefs we are holding.

Sit in a quiet place and take a few deep cleansing breaths.

▶ Then gently ask yourself:

Why am I not experiencing (the promotion, the relationship, the apartment I've been looking for)?

Why don't I have (enough money, enough time, enough help with)?

Why aren't I experiencing (Health, Joy, Perfect Relationship, etc…)?…..

Let the answers come without holding back.

▶ Write down the thoughts or phrases that come to you.

These answers are our egoic beliefs. Usually we can hear the voices of our parents, grandparents, siblings, coaches, teachers, friends, bosses and employees, and the ever present news and social media.

▶ Look at any negative or limiting beliefs, be grateful for the lessons they have brought you, then turn them into positive and powerful statements. For example:

If the belief is that I have to save for a rainy day (an unfortunate event), I can reframe that to: I am grateful for the ideas of saving that have supported me. I now choose to save for my empowerment. I always have enough and more than enough money. I choose to save for (a new house, car, vacation, retirement) that will empower me.

If the belief is that the world is a scary place, I can reframe that to: I am grateful for the attention to worldly events that I grew up with, but I no longer choose to see events as bad. I look forward to living life fully, and I know I am supported by the Universe. Life is always supportive of me, therefore nothing can be against me.

▶ Use your powerful affirmations to replace the previous thoughts of lack or limitation.

Change the voices in your head so they reflect your enlightened awareness.

Take Another Moment: Practice Mindfulness to Find What's Lurking Underneath

This mindfulness practice will uncover some treasure, and perhaps some trash.

▸ Take one of your daily activities: brushing your teeth, putting on sunscreen, money habits (saving or spending beliefs), eating habits.

▸ Ask yourself:

Where does this habit come from? Where did I learn it? Who taught it to me?

When did I first decide to do this practice? How old was I? When did it become a routine?

Now ask WHY did it become a routine? What was the reasoning, the thoughts behind the activity? Try to be specific. (Do you brush your teeth to have clean healthy teeth or so that you don't get cavities? Do you save in case there is a future tragedy, a rainy day, or because you feel empowered?) What are the underlying thoughts that have driven the development of these habits?

▸ Write down the habits and the old thoughts that are silently behind them.

▸ Next, cross out the old, negative reasoning and create a new empowering reason for your habit.

▶ Each day, as you do the usual activity, such as brushing your teeth, remind yourself of the empowered reason behind it.

CHAPTER 15

Be the Change

When Gandhi said, "Be the change you wish to see in the world," he was actually stating a spiritual Law: We attract what we *are*! Not what we *want*, but what we *ARE*. That is why when we speak our words, we back them with our passion and our emotions; we embody them knowing that what we are being, the way we are being, is what we are attracting. Our energy and vibration is attracting the energy and vibration of the situations, events, and circumstances that will match.

Once again, it isn't a matter of *when* I will manifest change, or *if* I will manifest change. Look all around you, everything you see is what you have manifested so far! You are creating and manifesting with your thoughts, feelings, and emotions right now. They have become the essence of who you are in this moment. When we wish to experience change, we go back to the beginning, the word, or gnosis, or blueprint, and we choose again. What we wish to change, we must embody first.

When I was young, I wanted to change the world. I

thought it was such a noble cause. As I discovered these practices, I realize just how difficult changing the world and everyone in it would be! Instead, I could turn my attention to myself. I could change myself. That seemed like a more reasonable endeavor.

"If you don't like something, change it; if you can't change it, change your attitude."

—MAYA ANGELOU

Until now, no one has taught us that we are here to create the life we want to live. If you're like me, our parents didn't teach us these truths. My parents taught me what they learned: that life is hard, that I'd have to work hard, find a good job, be smart, be lucky. I mean, how do you "be lucky"?! Our teachers didn't teach us this. I went to Catholic school and learned the opposite, that we are born with sin and have to beg and plead our way into God's good graces and maybe we will experience heaven when we die. Then again, maybe we wouldn't. No one was talking about experiencing the kingdom of Heaven, experiencing our enlightened state, right here, right now. I didn't learn it in college either; that was all about making the grade to get a good job, winning in sports, getting the degree, all to put you through to the next level. The next level of what?

I, and possibly you, grew up with these limiting beliefs, and much of the world is in agreement: the news media, social media, the political climate, and economic indicators. Even churches and religions have long-held beliefs that we are not here to experience or create paradise but to learn life's hard lessons, or that God is, for some reason, testing us to see if we are good enough. I could never have imagined that *I* was supposed to create the changes I wished to see in my life, changes in my situations, events, and circumstances, and my destiny.

Thankfully, I've learned that right now, this moment, is when I can make a change. I can decide in this moment to create the changes I want to see! I turn within, embody the quality, speak my word, know absolutely the Law is receiving and saying yes to me, and I joyfully create. I am the change!

What is the only thing standing in the way of creating our heaven on earth? Our own limiting perceptions and beliefs, our ego, our conditioning, our self-imposed ideas of lack. The only thing in the way of creating heaven on earth is our thoughts. They become our limits on how much good we will actually allow into our lives. Our thoughts become walls surrounding us and they contain blocks of limiting beliefs. What are some limiting thoughts that you grew up with, and the world agrees with? Life is hard? There is never enough time? Money doesn't grow on trees?

As we've discussed, we are creatures of habit and many of these thoughts and limiting beliefs have turned into behaviors and habits that we stick with long past their serving us. And what's the definition of insanity? Doing the same thing over and over again? What are you doing over and over again, expecting a different result? Sometimes the appropriate question may be, what are you *not* doing? Is there something that you really know in your heart would make for great and wonderful changes in your life, but you've talked yourself out of it? Do you subscribe to the adage that "change is hard?" Is change hard? Or is it the idea that "change is hard" that makes change hard? Change is just different.

When we know that life is forever changing, we can stop trying to hold on to things the way they are. We trust that whatever is next is perfect for whatever we need on this grand expedition. When we are living in the present moment, we embrace the journey, rather than clinging to any aspect of it.

"All that you touch, you change.
All that you change, changes you."
—OCTAVIA E. BUTLER

Spirit is forever growing, unfolding and expanding as form; we can just look in the mirror to know for certain that life in this world is constantly changing and change is the only constant. Living enlightened, we begin to fully participate in creating the changes we wish to see in the world, rather than be subjected to the random changes around us.

Create Change, or Allow Change to Create You!

Knowing intellectually and emotionally that life is all about change, that Spirit is forever unfolding in its expression of itself, that no two sunrises will ever be the same, we can learn to embrace change, to actually look forward to change and learn to create it rather than waiting for it to happen to us. When we feel the tug of our Spirit push us toward change, pay attention! When we realize that God is forever seeking a greater expression of Itself, we know that Spirit is seeking a greater expression through *us!*

So, let's look for a greater expression of ourselves. Maybe we need to stop taking our relationship for granted or take some classes that prepare us for a promotion at work. Perhaps we need to rethink our financial situation or prepare now for retirement. What is Spirit calling you to grow into?

"The world as we have created it is a process of our thinking. It cannot be changed without changing our thinking."

−ALBERT EINSTEIN

Breathe into Change

When change happens unexpectedly, we will often experience the rantings of the ego-mind. Flight-or-flight will kick in. The ego is screaming danger, run, fight, hide. This is the ego's job; it is there to protect the human body and mind and emotions, and it doesn't usually like change *at all.*

When we become aware of the ego voices, the tightening in our gut, the tensing of our shoulders, we know it's time to turn within. When the ego is yelling at us to not just sit there, DO something, we respond by saying, "I am. I am turning within right now. I am opening myself up to all possibilities right now. I am remembering the Truth of my Being right now, but thank you, ego, for bringing this to my attention." Breathe, and accept and allow the feelings of being overwhelmed or being fearful, and then allow them to pass as they surely will. The Truth of who we are shines into and through every situation, bringing about perfect change.

When we face change, whether expected or unexpected, we may only see a few opportunities and we may think they only range from bad to worse. Spirit is never limited. When we take a moment to relax into the Unlimited Possibility of Spirit in the silence of meditation, we make sense of the changes; we invite inspiration, and we allow channels to open up to us that may not have seemed like options before.

As humans, we get very comfortable with our routines. Routines make our ego feel as if we have control over our lives; they add meaning and a sense of timing. Sometimes they are little rituals that we do, like making that perfect cup of Earl Grey in the morning or stopping by Starbucks for the usual on our way to work.

When change comes unexpectedly, when we lose a job, or the kids go off to college, often it disrupts our routines. The pandemic came fast and hard and it forced us into many changes, big and small. It annihilated our routines and our sense of comfort and security.

The enlightened know that true comfort and security come from within; the ego doesn't know that. To fully integrate spirit, mind, and body, we take the time to create new routines and rituals based on the changes. Don't just stay in your pajamas, ordering takeout and pizza, because you feel a sense of desperation. Create and claim new rituals so that you can reclaim the sense of comfort that allows you to feel normal in your humanity. Take care of yourself—don't let the Thai take-out boxes pile up!

Change is also an important invitation to try something new! Yes, find some rituals that make you happy and give your mind and body a sense of comfort, but now is the time to try new things. Look for new opportunities; volunteer, take an online art class, a music class, a writing class, surf lessons. Work with teens, adults, homeless, or those in recovery. Sign up to teach music, or art, or poetry. Remember that if Life is for us, there can be no one and no thing against us. Who has said that you can't do these things? Be bold. Jump out of a plane, if thats something you've always wanted to do. Or create a community garden, if that's more your speed. Cultivate the Zen mind, beginner's mind, which means there is so much that is fresh and new for us and we can be inspired like children to learn new things. Be open to all of Life's possibilities, rather than focused on what has changed.

Often when change happens, we hear from all the well-meaning friends, family, neighbors, the media, and others that things are not good, that this change is bad! There aren't enough jobs, opportunities, that you're not qualified, you're over-qualified, you're too young or too old, or just not the right fit; that there are no good women, no good men, the good ones are all taken. People will want you to join the club of Negaholics. You get what you say yes to. Just say No. Turn within, be still, and know: Where you are is the perfect unfoldment of God's great good.

An old Chinese proverb reminds us that when the winds of change blow, some people build walls while others build windmills. Change is an opportunity of power, of expansion, of growth, and we can create the changes we wish to see by *embodying* the Good that we realize we are.

"Your brain will work tirelessly to achieve
the statements you give your subconscious
mind. And when those statements are
the affirmations and images of your goals,
you are destined to achieve them!"

—JACK CANFIELD

Part of creating change is becoming grateful for the insights and the stillness, for the rituals that give us a sense of calmness, for the new things, for our faith, for the words and actions of our spiritual teachers who embody our faith. Be grateful that we can actually plan out change, create our change, and reinvent ourselves all the time. By embracing change, we enjoy the journey and worry less about the destination and we live enlightened.

Take a Moment: Create Change

From right where we are, we can create the changes we wish to see in our lives. We become the change, and by becoming it, we call it forth into expression and form.

Take a few deep centering breaths, and with eyes closed, gently ask yourself, "What are some changes I wish to create in my Life?" Look into your health, your relationships, your self-expression in a job or career or retirement, your friendships, more vacation time, a more active lifestyle, a calmer lifestyle.

▸ Write down one change you wish to create in your life right now.

▸ Now, write down the limiting beliefs that popped up around creating this change, things you may have worked on before, or completely new fears, limiting thoughts, or beliefs, perhaps based on your family history, your past history, or the predicted economic condition. (It might be something like: "I don't have enough training," or "I'll never be able to qualify for a house.")

▸ Take a moment to rewrite your limiting beliefs as statements of Truth, something you are willing to believe, something you are willing to adopt as your new way of creating, and write it as an affirmation. Such as, "I am perfectly prepared for this promotion."

▸ Spend time embodying the affirmation; feel what it feels like to accomplish this goal. Breathe into the changes you are creating. Experience it now as if it were already done. Live in this moment as if it is done according to your belief.

▶ Close your eyes and ask, What do I have to *do*—what actions can I take—to create the changes I would like to see in my life? What gesture, ritual, or routine can I start doing to support this change in my life? What habits do I need to stop to support the changes I want to create in my life? What must I stop participating in to align myself with my highest Good? (Perhaps you take on some extra tasks at work, if you had the responsibilities already.)

▶ Write down one or two actions that you can take to align with the changes you wish to create in your life.

Feel and sense the power within you to create the changes you wish to see. Spirit knows nothing of big and small. Only our ego relates to things as easy or hard, worthy or unworthy. Step out of the ego and into Wholeness and feel the change as already complete!

Take Another Moment: Create a Vision Board of Change

A vision board is a fun way to envision and be inspired by the changes you are creating in your life. Gather the materials to make a fun collage reflecting the changes you desire from the previous exercise. Find photos, magazine clippings, quotes, book titles, song lyrics, images of yourself living these fresh changes. Use drawings, poetry, clip art, anything that inspires you. Organize these on a poster board or corkboard and place the board somewhere you will see it and be inspired every day.

Sit in front of your vision board for 10 minutes each day. Repeat the affirmations that inspire you from the vision board. *Feel* yourself already reveling in the wonderful changes you have created. Remember to BE THE CHANGE!

CHAPTER 16

Choose Love

Love is the creative power of the Universe. Love is the absence of separation. Love has no opposite. Fear is not its opposite, because Love is real and fear is simply the lack of awareness of Love. As a metaphor, we could also say that there is only darkness and light, but only light is real. Darkness is simply the absence of light shining on it.

"There are only two emotions: love and fear.
All positive emotions come from love,
all negative emotions from fear. From love
flows happiness, contentment, peace, and joy."

—ELIZABETH KÜBLER-ROSS

When we shine light on a shadow, the shadow disappears and we realize it was never real; it had no substance and did not exist on its own. In this metaphor, the light is eternal.

When we speak of Love as the great essence of Spirit, we are not speaking of romantic love, not a personal or physical love of someone or something, not love as an emotion, but the Loving Energy that created the heavens and earth, the galaxies, and stars, the Love that created us in Its image and likeness. From John 1, we know that "Perfect Love casts out all fear." What is Perfect Love? The unconditional love of Life Itself. It is a love without conditions, without expectations, without restrictions or barriers, without judgments, without fear. Perfect Love is all-inclusive and rejects nothing. It is the love of the All, rather than the love of the ego. It is the path to Wholeness and Oneness.

Fear Blocks Love and Creative Energy

We block the path of Creative Energy when we are in fear. The ego produces fear. It is a reaction and a resistance to outside threats to our body, our body of affairs, or our psyche. Fear is a natural part of human existence; it is a signal to look at a situation or event and discern if it will harm us or if we need to pay attention. When fear rises, we look at it and we must decide what it is telling us. When we react from the place of fear, we can limit ourselves. When we make decisions from Love, from Wholeness and not fear, we bring peaceful resolutions to our situations and relationships.

If there is a rattlesnake in my living room, I would sense fear and the fight-or-flight reflex within my body would kick in. It would only take a moment to discern the threat to myself, my son, and the dog. By breathing and responding, rather than reacting to the fear, I would intuit what would be best to do in the situation. Several friends have called me to remove snakes and spiders from their houses or garages because I have managed my fear of them! How does one manage their fear of snakes, you ask? For me, it was easy. In college, I had an 8-foot pet boa constrictor.

When we experience fear of losing our job or of physical abuse, the fear can get trapped in our body and can become consistent and subconscious. We can experience other fears such as not being able to pay the rent every month, bills piling up, or losing the affection of a loved one, which can overwhelm our physical and emotional bodies.

When we meditate and connect with our Selves as love, as peace, as abundance, when we recognize the Truth of our being, we let go of fear; it dissolves under the light of love. We can then sense how to resolve issues of bills piling up, relationships crumbling, and anything else in our realm of affairs.

When we shift our energy from fear to love, miracles happen. When we shift from fear to love, synchronicity happens. When we step into and fully embrace ourselves as the expression of God, of Love, we experience the kingdom of Heaven, and peace happens.

"If you knew the secret of life, you too would choose no other companion but love."

—RUMI

One of the first times I experienced this powerful love was the first moment that I found out I was pregnant. I fell in love! For the first time in my life, I experienced a completely unconditional love for someone. There were no conditions, because this little life inside of me had made no promises. There were no promises to be good, to grow up and be kind, to listen, to obey, to pick up his room, to stay clean, to eat his veggies, to be smart and make good grades. This little life was not even making promises to come out and make himself known. But there I was, truly, madly, deeply in love.

Soon after my son was born, I had this amazing revelation: This powerful, unconditional love I felt for him, this overwhelming love, is how we are supposed to love everyone. This is the love Jesus spoke about. This was how we are supposed to love our neighbor as ourselves. This is the loving compassion that Buddhism teaches, and the Sufis write about. This is the love of God for all of humanity, for all Its creations.

I remembered a Cold War song written by Sting, called, "I Hope the Russians Love Their Children Too." And I thought yes, the Russians do love their children too! And the Australians, and Africans, and South Americans, and Egyptians. I realized that the Catholics, Protestants, Jews, Muslims, Kabbalists, Buddhists, Jainists, Toaists, the Democrats, and Republicans, and the Independents, they all love their children too. A mother's love knows no boundaries, political, cultural, or religious. A mother's love is unconditional. I felt intuitively that Spirit's Love is unconditional and it is everywhere available. It is always ours to choose.

The Divine Creator created all of humanity, all life on the planet, the planet itself. This Creator hung the sun, the moon, and the stars, created galaxies and the Universe—and the Power of Its creation is Unconditional Love. Having my son has taught me the power of unconditional love.

> "There are two basic motivating forces: fear and love.
> When we are afraid, we pull back from life.
> When we are in love, we open to all that life has to
> offer with passion, excitement, and acceptance."
>
> —JOHN LENNON

Fear is Misguided Faith

I've explained how I have come to understand the power of Unconditional Love; now I'll talk about fear.

I moved back to my hometown after a divorce when my son was 2. I was reveling in being home again, experiencing through the eyes of my son the things I experienced when I grew up at the beach in Florida. I was so happy! I was free! I had no job, a beautiful new house in a lovely neighborhood, a beautiful 2-year-old boy; we were going to the beach every day, and we didn't have a care in the world. We were free and happy. And then one morning, I woke up and I realized, "I have no job, a big new house, I'm a single mom of a beautiful 2-year-old boy, and here I am going to the beach every day. What am I thinking?"

For the first time in my life, I felt a new fear, panic even, the fear of being completely responsible for this other little life; I felt so so small and helpless. All of my doubts and fears came crashing to the surface of my daily life. I could only see my present circumstance. I could only see with my eyes that what was in my bank account seemed to have dissolved into thin air. I could only hear what was happening in the world of effects—the shrinking of the stock market, the real estate market, the job market—and it terrified me. I believed I was so limited due to my lack of credentials and experience in any sort of job market, much less the crash that was taking place in the news every day.

After exhausting myself a few times, I woke up in the middle of the night once again, and instead of crying, instead of regretting and resenting and panicking as I had already done, somehow I remembered the place where Spirit resides, where God is, and I turned within. I stayed in meditation and prayer until dawn. I prayed to a god outside myself, because in that moment everything was outside myself, and I asked, "What would you have me do? I, of myself, can do nothing."

It was in the realization that I, of myself, my small, little, fearful, doubtful self, could do nothing, I remembered in God all things are possible. It felt good. I heard and I remembered, "I and my Father, the Creator, are one" and it felt good. I remembered that "it is done to you as you believe," and it felt good, because I could remember that God is good. Life is good, Spirit is powerful, Love is transformative. And I realized that I had simply misplaced my faith. I had placed my faith in the world of effects, in the world of precedent, in the external world of forms. In that moment, my vision came back: I am my Source revealed. God, Spirit, all of Life is for me and my limiting, fearful thoughts are the only thing against me. And I can change those. I can choose again.

Fear, no matter how palpable, may not be real, but it is a wake-up call. My overwhelming fear was a wake-up call to the next stage in my life and that big changes were coming. I needed to get to the bottom of fear, to explore it and realize its temporal nature, so that I could let it go and fully participate in the creative flow of my life. It reminded me to choose wisely: be in fear or allow the Creative Love energy to run my life!

"Faith allows us to perceive the invisible,
believe in the incredible, and receive the impossible."
—REV. ARTHUR CHANG

Sometimes we work so hard to bring things and situations into our lives; we want to bring prosperity, health, love, or success into our lives, but we end up working against the flow. When we are in the flow of Life, we release these things from within, we reveal the Truth that is already within us. We unblock the flow of loving, creative energy that we *are*—and we release these things AS ourself, into our lives. We reveal from within the health, joy, peace, and prosperity that we already are. We have already been given the gifts, because we have already inherited the Kingdom.

We are always at a point of choice. We can choose to feed the voice of fear, or we can feed the voice of love and creative energy. It is so simple when we realize the power of our choice. We are Love. We have an abundance to give and to share. There is never a moment that Spirit is not trying to speak love, kindness, and compassion through us. In every situation, we have the ability to choose more and more love.

At the doctor's office, paying bills, in line at the post office, when we eat, when we vote, when we pray, when we walk—in every thought, every action, every response, every word, we can choose love because we are Love.

The world needs our love. There is no power on earth greater than the power of love. When we align with the Love we are, we experience the condition of the universe supporting us, of unique events coming into fruition; we experience a flow in our lives. And we remember that we can choose Love rather than feed fear.

"One of the first things to do is to love everybody.
If you have not done this, begin to do so at once."

—ERNEST HOLMES

I smile every time I think of this quote. Now, go and love everyone right this minute!

Take a Moment: Choose Again

This is a great evening meditation. When we lovingly review our day, we can see moments where we might have chosen love, rather than fear. We can return to these moments and shine the light of love on them now.

▸ Take a few minutes to go over your day as honestly and unattached as possible. See some moments where you were calm, joyful, present, alert, grateful, or powerful. Really feel how your body felt in these moments and how your environment seemed at these moments. Just enjoy this for a few minutes.

▶ Now turn your attention to a time in your day you may not have been as enlightened as you may have wanted to be. Is there a moment, an event where you could have been more loving, more compassionate? Did you react to a news event, social media post, or cancelled appointment? Gently see the event happening as unattached as possible.

▶ Gently ask yourself, "How could I choose Love in this situation? Can I feel empathy, compassion? Can I imagine a whole new scenario unfolding in which my love pours into this situation and changes it completely?" Rest in this new vision.

▶ Allow yourself to relive the situation with love, compassion, and understanding. Experience the light of Love shining on it, through it, and through you.

When we remember how powerful love is, we will choose it every time. There is no greater transformational power, and it is at our fingertips right now and every day.

CHAPTER 17

Be the Tree

Have you ever been to Colorado, or Utah and walked amongst the aspen groves? Aspens are interesting and unique trees, with their white bark with dark spots, and their leaves are slightly rounded, shaped like little fans. When the wind blows, they shake and make a crisp, rattling sound. But the most interesting thing about aspens is that they are not separated from each other. They do not have a separate root system. They are all connected from underneath by a root system that we cannot see. In this root system, there are little shoots, new life springing up, saplings, mature trees, and even old and dying members making room for the new growth.

There are so many, and so much, that make up the ONE.

—ELIZABETH CANTEY

Aspen trees are not separate and apart from each other. They are all connected under the earth. They are individual, they are different, *and* they are connected. If anything should happen to one tree or several, it could potentially spread to each and every tree. Interesting word, "individual". The word originally derives from the word "indivisible": the word individual means "indivisible from the whole." There is a grove of over 47,000 aspens near the Fishlake National Forest in Utah that scientists believe is the largest living organism on the planet! Hmmmmm.

Connections

Do you know the phrase, "There, but for the grace of God, go I?" I remember my grandmother used to say it. When someone says it, it usually means that whatever unfortunate circumstances the other person is experiencing, it is just by the grace of God that I am not experiencing them as well. If someone is very sick or dying, we might say that phrase and count our blessings of health. If our friend lost their job and was struggling to find a new one and pay the bills, we might use that phrase and be grateful for our job, our income.

One day I was walking by a homeless man. He was in pretty bad shape. Terrible shape. That phrase, in the voice of my grandmother, popped into my head. As it formed in my mind, the words shifted and what I heard was, "There, *because* of the grace of God, go I." I was instantly connected to this man. I experienced a deep sense of oneness and kinship, and I instantly knew he and I were connected by something that neither of us could see. I knew we were one in Source, and we were individual yet indivisible from the whole that is

Spirit. I am there in that homeless man.

The experience of oneness continued for a while as I felt myself uniquely connected to everyone I saw and imagined. There I am as the single mom, as the schoolteacher, the artist, the junkie, the teenager. I am who thou art, and thou art who I am. I am right there. I am there in the pop star and the paparazzi. There I am as the salesman who lost his job, the teenager who's lost her way, the politician, the religious leader, the dying, the shaman, the mystic, the newborn. I experienced the mystical Oneness that connects us all. We are all One Life expressing. In every person, there because of the grace of God, go I.

"We may ignore, but we can nowhere evade
the presence of God. The world is crowded with
Him. He walks everywhere incognito."

—C.S. LEWIS

Forget the aspens, *WE* are the largest living organism on the planet!

WE are all connected by something we cannot see. What happens to one of us can potentially happen to each and all of us. We are One Life expressed individually and indivisible from the Whole.

When we experience our divine Oneness, our kinship with all life, we see the Truth of the world in which we live and we grow as one global family that respects and honors the interconnectedness of all life on the planet. We recognize ourselves in the other, and we see the face of God everywhere we go.

Buddhism acknowledges the interdependence of all life. Nothing exists on its own; everything exists only as it is connected to everything else. It is One expressing as All, and no thing has a separate existence. Existence is only in the connection, or unity. Buddhism has a saying: Treat everyone as if they were your mother, because they could have been your mother in a past life! In the Christian bible, we are told to love our neighbor as ourself. In Kabbalah, the law is seen as "Love your neighbor because *you are* your neighbor; you and your neighbor participate in a mystical oneness." This changes everything.

I See You

The greatest gift we can give anyone is our attention. We can notice them, the Truth of their Being, and remember they are a part of us, and we them. "Sawubona" is an African Zulu greeting that generally means "I see you." It has much more depth and nuance than our traditional "hi' or "hello." It means, "I see your personality. I see your humanity. I see your dignity. I respect you." In the African village context, where everyone knows one another, it starts every conversation with a powerful sense of Oneness and communion.

The traditional answer someone gives to the aforementioned greeting is "Ngikhona." It translates as, "I am here," but it's more complex. It tells the greeter that you feel seen and understood, that your personal essence is recognized. Inherent in the Zulu greeting and the grateful response is the sense that until you saw me, I didn't exist. By recognizing me, I know who I am and there is meaning in my life.

This invocation has several unique components. First, it begins with two people looking deep into each other's eyes. This is powerful by itself. It establishes a depth of connection without any words. Eye contact is soul contact. When we connect on the soul level, we communicate on the soul level; we understand on the soul level and not just with our words. Second, "I see you" tells the person that you see them as an integrated Being, as a divine emanation of Spirit, and as the unique human being they are. You recognize them, and they are a part of you. It is an invitation to be authentic, open, and honest. And saying "I am here" is a declaration of intent to completely inhabit this moment, to be present. It is a willingness to be honest, in integrity, and compassionate. It means "I will be authentically me and allow you to be wholly you."

This greeting represents the Zulu philosophy of ubuntu, which translates roughly as "humanity toward all." Ubuntu is a spiritual ethic that advocates mutual support for "bringing each other into existence." It implies that we work together for the collective good, rather than the good of the individual. We know we are all connected. In Hinduism, this is described as seva, or selfless service. It means to be in service for the good of the whole rather than the few or the individual.

I encourage you, the next time you meet someone, to greet them wholeheartedly. Take a moment to reflect consciously and actually "see" the person. Notice their unique physical character and traits, as well as who they are beyond the physical. They, like you, are a child of the Most High.

When we truly see another, we honor and respect them. We shine our divine light upon them, a spiritual light that is both energizing and empowering. This is so simple. We meet and greet people every day, but do we, in reality, take a moment to see the magnificence within them when we say hello? If not, this is actually a reflection of ourselves because often we don't see or recognize our own magnificence. Only when we actually "see" ourselves and acknowledge our own inner divinity that we have the capacity to recognize this in another.

The enlightened do one thing first in any situation, they show up. The enlightened claim their identity and understand through experience that all people are connected. To live enlightened, we have to be willing to show the world who we are so that we reflect back to them the truth of who they are. And we have to keep showing up despite any setbacks or stumbling blocks. The temptation to edit ourself and to hide our light will only leave us feeling disconnected, small, and wanting. The more authentic we are, the more alive we feel. And as we are lifted in consciousness, all are lifted. There is only One.

"We are all connected. To each other, biologically.
To the earth, chemically.
To the rest of the universe, atomically."

—NEIL DEGRASSE TYSON

Take a Moment: Truly See

When we spiritually see the other, we give them the greatest gift: recognizing the Truth of their Being. Use this greeting every day for a week and watch how it transforms everyday experiences into enlightened ones. You don't need to use the words of the Zulu greeting, of course, but incorporate the intention of the greeting into your "hello" or "how are you." Set your intention to really see the others in your life today and every day.

▶ Consciously greet everyone you see today, from the trash collector to the banker, your children, employees, the grocery store clerk.

▶ Look into the other's eyes. Eye contact is soul contact. If they are too busy, that's ok; it is your intention that matters most. Say "hello," or "how are you," or "thank you" intending to see the Truth about the person right in front of you. See them as family.

▶ As you recognize them, notice a Divine quality in them, their beauty, kindness, patience, wisdom, preparedness, efficiency, etc. You may be able to let them know that you can see this about them. Have the intention of being a powerful presence of Love for them.

▶ When someone greets you, say hello back with the full intention of being authentic and being seen. Just be present. If someone asks how you are, tell them how you are, not just a rote answer and not the story about how you are.

We are one family, one race, and our language is the language of Love. See if you can recognize how you are related to others in our human family. Remember, it isn't about the words; it is about a soul-to-soul connection. And do not worry if the others cannot look at you or are too busy to respond; it is about what you do and your intention to reveal the Truth in every situation.

CHAPTER 18

The Ultimate Law of Attraction

We are here to surround ourselves with Love and Joy the likes of which may have only been revealed to us so far in brief, fleeting moments. We are meant to live our every moment in that Love, in that Joy. How do we attract such Joy and Bliss, Abundance and Creativity?

In chapter 8, we looked briefly at the Law of Attraction as it relates to the creative process, and as you recall, the Law of Attraction is like energy or a vibration that attracts or draws to itself similar energy and vibration. What that means is that we are constantly attracting WHAT WE ARE. Our thoughts and feelings are indicators of what we are attracting.

Feeling joyful, confident, loving always brings to us more situations and opportunities to feel even more joy, more confidence, and more love. When we are focused on what we don't have—not enough money, not enough, time, not enough peace—we attract to ourselves more situations, events, and circumstances to reflect the not-enoughness in our life. We attract WHAT WE ARE in this moment and not what we wish for.

We are here on earth in form to create our personal and unique paradise; we are here to *experience* heaven on earth. Universal Law absolutely works on our behalf, but only as we are familiar with it, practice it, and demonstrate it. We, as humans, learned about the laws of nature: gravity, buoyancy, aerodynamics, etc. We learned how to cooperate and work with them to improve our life experiences here on earth. We learned to walk on the moon, float on ships, and fly around the world. So too can we learn about the Universal Laws or Spiritual Laws and deeply enhance our life, attracting into our life everything we would like to experience.

We have had many teachers throughout the ages come to show us the way. At times, their message has been distorted, corrupted, and lost. But there are some powerful Truths which remain and this is one of them:

"Seek first the Kingdom of Heaven and all else will be added to you."

—MATTHEW 6:33

The Key

When you feel your alignment with Spirit and you are experiencing it in all that you do, expressing it in your work, in your family, and your body, your life-force becomes supercharged. Your thoughts are no longer the weak, limiting thoughts of the ego: fears of the future, regrets about the past, judgments, and reactions; therefore, you are no longer attracting or experiencing fear, anxiety, or depression. You no longer attract situations which bring shame or regret. You've practiced forgiveness, peace, and being present in each moment. You've learned to be still and to be inspired. You've learned to choose and choose again.

Awakened, you now attract new, inspired, enlightened activity into your life. The people who come into your life are living at a higher vibration and attracting higher good to themselves as well. There is more Joy, Peace, Love, and Abundance showing up in your life because you are all these qualities of Spirit, and you are attracting people, situations, events, and ideas that bring more and more of these qualities into your life. As you seek first the kingdom of Heaven, answers, ideas, relationships, finances, ALL is added to you.

So what exactly is the kingdom of Heaven? For some like myself who grew up in Christian religions, it would mean that we are to search for and put first a realm of angels with white wings playing gold harps floating on clouds of silver. That never really works, does it? Not only do I not feel compelled to search out this sort of heaven, but how in the world would I put it first? Thankfully, the keys to unlocking this truth are also in the words of Jesus. He said the kingdom of Heaven is at hand now. And the kingdom of Heaven is within. Sound familiar?

The kingdom of Heaven is a state of consciousness in which we experience our Oneness and Wholeness, a felt innate Oneness with All There Is. It is the integration of spirit, mind, and body. The kingdom of Heaven is enlightenment! We could say: Seek first enlightenment, a state of conscious awareness of Oneness, and all else will be added to you!

Seek

We are told that just seeking the kingdom of Heaven, our enlightenment, is enough to grant us access to All Else. Jesus did not demand that we be in the kingdom, or *master* the kingdom, or *remain constantly* in the kingdom of Heaven, the state of consciousness that is enlightenment. We are told that the practice of seeking will put us in a state of consciousness that reveals our true Spiritual Identity. We are Spiritual Beings having a human experience, and the act of seeking our true identity will shift our human experiences into an awareness where answers come from an unlimited and unprecedented Source. Seek, and all will be added.

Seek First

We are informed to seek first, not second or third, the kingdom, the consciousness. Seek, first and foremost, enlightenment and All Else will be added to us. While we are focused on developing the qualities of the Divine in us—Love, Joy, Peace, and Abundance—we are attracting these qualities through all of our human experiences. When we are committed to living in the present moment, transcending the ego, letting go of the past, not projecting into the future, we are raising our vibration and attracting better and higher and more loving experiences into our life. We aren't told to seek first our perfect relationship and all else will be added, or seek first the perfect job, or even our perfect self-expression. Why worry and fret constantly over all our human structures—our home, work, relationships, our health—when we are told that seeking first our enlightened state will elicit all of our good in every area of our life.

If we practice seeking first enlightenment in all our endeavors, when a crisis occurs, we will turn inward to the Source of all our good, our creativity, the Source of knowledge and wisdom, and be guided and directed to which solution is best. We find a harmony with whatever is, which in turn, leads to more and more enlightened living. We can seek first from right where we are, in the midst of crisis, when we want a new job, a new relationship, or financial abundance. We can seek first our state of felt Oneness, and we are assured that what we need and desire most will be added. Live enlightened and watch your paradise unfold before your eyes.

The Kingdom of Heaven

The kingdom of Heaven is not a place. We will not find it with signs pointing to it. We are told it is within; it is a state of consciousness in which we know and experience the Eternal Essence pouring through us, as us, flowing into everything we do, and surrounding us with All That It Is. The kingdom of Heaven is our enlightened state, which has already been given us. As we've discovered, enlightenment is something we can experience directly by focusing on this present moment, right now. When we put our attention on the simple task at hand, doing the dishes, returning an email, buying groceries, or just breathing, we sense a connection with our spirit, our mind, our body, and everything around us. We can sense and feel the Eternal Essence in all that we are and all that we do. There is a peace and inherent calm in the present moment in which we feel connected to our Source and our Supply and our very Essence.

All Else

Not a little more, or something else, or enough, or only what you need will be added; ALL will be added! All Else includes all the human structures: home, work, relationships, finances, health, and spiritual enlightenment. When our human structures are growing and unfolding in a greater and greater expression of our good, we can give and contribute more to ourselves, our family, and our community. We connect powerfully to our Divine Purpose.

Our purpose, our authentic Nature, and anything and everything we need to fully express ourself in this beautiful life will be added. And just as our enlightenment is never stagnant; it is always changing, growing, shifting, and expanding, and so too will the All that is added to us change, expand, and unfold. As we step more and more into enlightenment, we attract all that we need to accomplish our purpose in life, easily and effortlessly.

When we live in the present moment and feel ourself enlightened in our activities, we reveal our creative nature, solve problems better, deal with upset and illness more easily, and create less suffering. All that we need to experience heaven on earth is freely given to us.

Will Be Added to You

It will be done to you. There is no efforting on your part. There is nothing you need to do to make this happen, or to make any law happen, for the Universe works with ease and in harmony within Itself. There is no effort to make gravity hold us to the earth, and we do not work to keep a plane in the sky when we understand the laws of aerodynamics.

"It's not your work to make anything happen.
It's your work to dream it and let it happen.
The Law of Attraction will make it happen.
In your joy, you create something, and then
you maintain your vibrational harmony with it,
and the Universe *must* find a way to bring it about.
That's the promise of the Law of Attraction."

—ESTHER HICKS

When you maintain the vibrational harmony with that which you desire, all that you want and need is added to you, flows to you, and expresses through you effortlessly. We attract everything we need through synchronicity, creative ideas, gifts, special relationships, and unexplained phenomena that others might call "luck." They might even call it a miracle, but it is just the Law in action. It becomes the norm for the one who seeks first her enlightenment.

Jesus doesn't claim that all will be added to you if you work very, very hard, or if you join this religious group, or if you meditate only this way, or if you visualize or affirm for five hours every day. As we seek first, all is simply added. The home that you want will appear in your circumstances and the way to make it yours will be added. As you seek first your enlightenment, imagine how your relationships will change and grow. Imagine how all the situations and circumstances you need to express your Self will flow to you through this Ultimate Law of Attraction.

The most important aspect of seeking first enlightenment is that as we step into the state of consciousness that allows us to experience ourselves as the Eternal Essence, we discern so more easily what we actually *want* to appear in our lives. We bypass all the wishing and wanting of superficial, material things that we *think* we want because we believe that they will satisfy our ego; instead we step into a space of Love, Joy, Peace, and Abundance and attract more situations and relationships that bring us real Love, Joy, Peace and Abundance. As we step consciously into the space of Wholeness, the need to satisfy the ego dissolves; there is no more competing with the Jones' or wondering what the next career move is. The way is shown, all is given, and all we need is to be open to receive.

We all have friends or relatives that are so determined to bring something or some*one* into their lives. They work hard using the Law of Attraction; they visualize the new relationship, the new promotion, the new "toy" that they must have, only to get the things they wanted and still not be satisfied. Sometimes these things are even very, very detrimental in their lives and a cause for great suffering. Yet, these people have used the Law of Attaction very well.

I had a dear friend who moved to Los Angeles when I did. He became best friends with several of my good friends. Mark was a successful businessman who had lots of high profile and famous clients. He lived on the ocean and loved extreme sports. He had used the power of creative thought to create a beautiful life. He was funny, healthy, wealthy, had friends and a job and created a company he loved. After his second divorce, Mark decided his next marriage would be to a younger woman who would want to have a child with him. His biggest regret was that he didn't have a child of his own, and he set that as his new goal. It didn't take him long to find a beautiful young woman and they quickly married and had their first child. As I said, he was adept and powerful when it came to the Law of Attaction!

We didn't see much of Mark after that. He got everything he wished for and more: the wife, the child, the continued success and financial security. Right after his wife announced that she was pregnant with their second child, Mark drove his beautiful red Ferrari off the cliffs on Mulholland Drive. He killed himself. It was devastating for his friends and his young family.

What went wrong? Mark had a list of things he thought would make him happy, but he was gravely mistaken. Mark forgot to ask to be happy. We often think we know what will make us happy and we work very hard mentally, emotionally and physically, to get those things. We tend to forget that what the ego wants and what the Spirit wants may be very, very different. The fleeting happiness that comes with acquiring material things cannot hold a candle to the brilliance of revealing the Joy of Spirit that is within.

The most powerful decision we could make is the decision to be joyful, peaceful, and abundant, and we attract to us all the situations, events, and circumstances that would bring us more joy, peace, and prosperity.

When we align ourselves with our highest good, and the highest good of everyone around us, we attract only good. When we align ourselves with our ego goals, we can never truly be satisfied. We may work hard to gain the things, situations, and events that satisfy the ego, and we may get everything we set our minds on, but these things cannot bring us lasting happiness. When we stand in Spirit, we are always guided and directed to our highest joy.

Attract what you want by *being what you want,* because we don't get what we want, we get what we ARE.

"We often become what we believe ourselves to be. If I believe I cannot do something, it makes me incapable of doing it. When I believe I can, I acquire the ability to do it, even if I didn't have it in the beginning."

—GANDHI

When we are living in our enlightenment, putting our attention on the kingdom of heaven, the state of consciousness of Oneness, imagine the frequency at which we are vibrating. There is nothing we cannot have or do. When we align ourselves with Life, when we integrate spirit, mind, and body, no thing and no one is against us. No wonder this is the ultimate Law of Attraction!

Your Moment to Realize

Turn within now and take a few deep breaths. Seek first, realize first, the truth of your Being.

You are not your body, you are the one experiencing your body.

You are not your thoughts, you are experiencing or knowing your thoughts.

You are not your past, your memories, your hopes, your dreams; you are the one experiencing those.

You are not an experience; you are the knower of experience.

You are the infinite vast space which is aware of all experience. As you breathe into yourself, you can sense your Reality as Oneness and Wholeness.

Everywhere you look, you "see" wholeness. You can see and sense the Truth behind all appearances.

Standing in Oneness, Wholeness, Love, and Creativity, you know that all is well, even in the mess, and you live a joyful, peaceful, and fulfilled life.

And so it is…

EPILOGUE

Realizing All is Well

When is a tree perfect? Have you ever wondered? As a seed? A sapling? A young tree? A mature full tree? Or when it is dying, decaying, and released back into the earth? Can a tree ever be perfect? The truth is, it is perfect at any given moment. Because at every given moment it is fully realized as a tree. It is whole, perfect, and complete at each and every moment because it is at its fullest potential for that moment!

Right Where We Are, Spirit Is, and All is Well

We are created whole, perfect, and complete. At any given moment we can realize our Wholeness. Our life becomes filled with Love, Joy, and Peace the instant we realize it is so. We can only realize it in the present moment, this moment, right now.

Often, we project our happiness into the future: "I'll be happy when I attract my perfect job or have enough money. I'll be happy when I find my soulmate. I'll be happy when I am enlightened." As soon as we project our happiness into the future, we've conceded that we cannot be happy right now. We are in essence saying to the All There Is, "I am not created whole—I will be whole when I finally attract these things which will make me feel whole."

We work hard, sometimes very hard, to attract those things we want. The dream job comes, and the perfect relationship comes, and the luxury vacation comes, and the recognition comes, and still we find that now, we need something else to make us feel whole. And we create another list of things we need to feel and be happy.

When we focus on the past, either trying to avoid past mistakes or trying to recapture what made us happy then, we are not able to experience our good now. We are telling the Universe, "I was happy then, and now I am not. I can't possibly be." We all know people who spend a lot of time living in "the good old days," and they cannot be in two places at the same time!

Living in the happiness or fear of the past prevents us from experiencing this perfect moment now.

We have learned that Joy, Beauty, and Peace are always available to us in everything we do. Right where we are, there is the infinite possibility for unbounded Joy, profound Peace, unconditional Love, and unlimited Abundance.

Acknowledging the integration of spirit, mind, and body in the present moment allows us to be fulfilled right where we are, right now. Until we realize, make real for ourselves, that we need nothing to make us whole, and we need no thing to complete us, we will search outside ourselves and forever be disappointed. So the cycle continues, until we stop and simply become Present to our Divine Essence right where we are.

Like the tree, we are Perfect in every moment of our life. The moment we realize this, it becomes true for each of us... We are living enlightened.